ISLAMIC AFRICA

VOLUME 4, ISSUE 2 FALL 2013

Northwestern University Press
Evanston, Illinois

www.islamicafricajournal.org

Scope and Mission: *Islamic Africa* is a peer-reviewed, multidisciplinary, academic journal published by Northwestern University Press in collaboration with the Institute for the Study of Islamic Thought in Africa (ISITA), based at Northwestern University, Evanston, Illinois. The journal incorporates *Sudanic Africa,* retaining its focus on historical sources, bibliographies, and methodologies. *Islamic Africa* promotes interaction between scholars of Islam and Africa across all continents and across historical periods. The journal welcomes papers from the humanities and the social sciences on any aspect of Islam and Muslim life pertaining to Africa, or originating from the African continent.

Communications concerning manuscripts and editorial matters should be addressed to Prof. Scott Reese, Editor, *Islamic Africa,* Northwestern University Press, 629 Noyes Street, Evanston, IL 60208 (USA); islamicafrica@northwestern.edu. For information about submitting manuscripts, see www.islamicafricajournal.org.

Concerning advertising and subscriptions, address the Managing Editor, Lauren Pretnar, Northwestern University Press, 629 Noyes Street, Evanston, IL 60208 (USA); islamicafrica@northwestern.edu. Electronic subscriptions can be purchased for institutions ($125) and individuals ($75) by visiting www.islamicafricajournal .org.

 ISSN 2154-0993.

Northwestern University Press acknowledges Marianne Jankowski for the interior design and Ahmad Faris for the journal logo. The copy editor for this issue was Paul Mendelson.

ISLAMIC AFRICA

ISLAMIC AFRICA
Incorporating SUDANIC AFRICA

Contents

ARTICLES

SOURCES

BOOK REVIEWS

Islamic Africa is a peer-reviewed, multidisciplinary, academic journal published by Northwestern University Press in collaboration with the Institute for the Study of Islamic Thought in Africa (ISITA), based at Northwestern University, Evanston. The journal incorporates *Sudanic Africa*, retaining its focus on historical sources, bibliographies, and methodologies. *Islamic Africa* promotes interaction between scholars of Islam and Africa across all continents and across historical periods. We welcome papers on any aspect of Islam and Muslim life pertaining to Africa and/or Africans from the humanities and the social sciences, especially those originating from the African continent.

ARTICLES

Imagining Arab Communities: Colonialism, Islamic Reform, and Arab Identity in Mombasa, Kenya, 1897–1933

Nathaniel Mathews, NORTHWESTERN UNIVERSITY

DOI: 10.5192/215409930402135

ABSTRACT

After the advent of British colonial rule, the epistemological prestige of Muslim culture, Arabic literacy, and qadi courts declined in Kenya. Coastal residents sought favorable court rulings outside qadi courts, which no longer had independent jurisdiction, and many sought education and jobs in a British colonial system less favorable to Islamic learning. Recognizing these challenges, Sheikh al-Amin Mazrui—Kenya's most prominent Islamic scholar—founded a newspaper called al-Islah in 1932. He was inspired by the prominent Cairo journal al-Manar, by the Salafi reformers Rashid Rida and Muhammad Abduh. Although al-Islah's themes were similar to al-Manar's in advocating for Islamic reform, al-Islah addressed itself to Swahili-speaking Arabs in a milieu where Muslims were increasingly a demographic minority and culturally marginalized. Print technology (al-Islah was printed in both Kiswahili and Arabic) and Salafi ideas in al-Islah worked together to spread reform and encourage East African Muslims to value Arabic and the pursuit of sharīʿa. Although these ideas were products of a long Islamic tradition that privileged access to knowledge as the passport of the believer, they were also newly self-conscious reflections of Arab cultural and religious identity; al-Islah's articles stressed the Arab role in creating Muslim civilization in Africa. Al-Islah critiqued the parochial na-

Islamic Africa, VOL. 4, NO. 2, 2013. ISSN 2154-0993. www.islamicafricajournal.org

ture of the British colonial project, urging a return to pre-colonial modes of Islamic hegemony and stressing the essential role of sharīʾa in constituting Islamic identity. Islamic reform in East Africa and the "re-imagination" of transnational Arab identity within it depended on Arab Muslims understanding the importance of Islamic knowledge—particularly Arabic and sharīʾa—in constituting coastal communities.

In the early twentieth-century coastal East African city of Mombasa, Kenya, the town's urban Arab elite faced a number of significant challenges to their prestige, reproduction, and rule as a dominant group.[1] The following article explores how they imagined their cultural and religious identity in response to British colonial modes of rule that transformed the epistemological prestige of Islam, redefined its social importance, and attempted to make "legible" the thickly complex social space of the Swahili coastal region. I focus on an Islamic newspaper called *al-Islah* (*Reform*), which was edited and published in Mombasa in the early 1930s and read widely by Swahili- and Arabic-speaking Muslims along the Kenyan coast and in Zanzibar. In relation to the economic processes reshaping the social space of Mombasa and the challenge of British colonialism to its Muslim elite, I discuss the social role of God's path/law (shariʾa) in *al-Islah,* narrate the anxiety of *al-Islah*'s writers and readers over its legal prestige in colonial Kenya, and explore the meaning of the term for the Arab community in Mombasa, Kenya.[2]

While roughly equivalent to Islamic law by Western definition, Shariʾa should be thought of in the pages of *al-Islah* as a "total social discourse where all kinds of institutions, not just Islamic law, find expression."[3] Thus, the call for shariʾa in *al-Islah* reflects a desire to return to the total pattern of life that existed when Islamic knowledge enjoyed a place of pride in the coastal knowledge economy, including both the legal sphere and the social principles that enabled the reproduction of this knowledge. Shariʾa as discursive trope in *al-Islah* encompassed both a transnational *geography* of Islamic reform and a local *genealogy* of knowledge, with

[1] Among the languages more widely spoken in Mombasa in the twentieth century were Swahili, Arabic, English, Gujarati, Katchchi, Urdu, Mijikenda, Luo, and Kikuyu.

[2] Arjun Appadurai, *Modernity at Large: Cultural Dimensions of Globalization* (Minneapolis: University of Minnesota Press, 1996), 189.

[3] Brinkley Messick, *The Calligraphic State: Textual Domination and History in a Muslim Society* (Berkeley: University of California Press, 1993), 3–4.

its origin point being the arrival of the first pious (Arab) ancestors (*wazee wetu*) to Mombasa's shores.[4] As such, the call within *al-Islah*'s pages for a return to the shariʾa itself draws on an imagination of Islam's role in Mombasa's past.

On the East African coast, the local language for centuries was Kiswahili, and it was lingua franca in the cultural spaces of a string of urban city-states on a stretch of coastline from Barawa in Somalia to Kilwa in southern Tanzania.[5] Traditionally, the Swahili city-states were able to integrate new migrants from both the Indian Ocean and the rural hinterland. These migrants came as slaves (*watumwa*), merchants, porters, scholars, and descendants of the Prophet Muhammad (*masharifu*), but Islam was a common cultural currency rooted in a coastal ideal of social refinement known as *uungwana,* which embodied gentility, generosity, and piety—the opposite of *ushenzi,* a term indicating barbarism, lack of civility, and non-Muslim origins.[6] Knowledge, family origin, and public social behavior were closely intertwined in the meaning and social resonance of these words. The *waungwana* (free urban elite) regarded themselves as the cultural superiors of their hinterland neighbors because of their social knowledge: literacy in Arabic, access to urban and international trading networks, and prestigious international origins. Social and linguistic knowledge were deployable symbols marking a kind of habitus denoting gentility, piety, and the totality of learned bodily skills, habits, education, and style. Since the early nineteenth century, with the advent of Busaidi rule over the coast, the terms to describe the social ideals of Islamic civilization on the Swahili Coast had grown more Arabo-centric, and the link between knowledge, Islam, and social prestige strengthened. The increasing importance in the

[4] Whether or not the point of origin for this imagination among the Arab elite is the seventh-century hegira, where the Prophet Muhammad establishes his rule in Medina and begins the process of "civilizing" the Arabs, or the bringing of Islam to East Africa by groups of Arab migrants in the following centuries is an interesting matter of discussion. Both events appear in *al-Islah* as milestones of Arab civilization.

[5] Michael Lambek, "Foreword," in *Struggling with History: Islam and Cosmopolitanism in the Western Indian Ocean,* ed. Kai Kresse and Edward Simpson (New York: Columbia University Press, 2008), xvii.

[6] Although *uungwana* was necessarily the antithesis of *ushenzi,* many enslaved people from the hinterlands converted to Islam, bought their freedom, or were eventually manumitted. The struggle of slaves and lower-class "plebeians" to lay claim to the social status of the *waungwana* has been described by Jonathan Glassman in *Feasts and Riot: Revelry, Rebellion and Popular Consciousness on the Swahili Coast, 1856–1888* (Portsmouth, N.H.: Heinemann/James Currey, 1995).

mid-nineteenth century of the term *ustaarabu* on the Swahili Coast exemplifies this connection between knowledge and social prestige; the term could mean both becoming knowledgeable and becoming Arab.[7]

The discursive language of the East African ulama was also based on this hierarchy of knowledge. A scholar's legitimacy was rooted in the control of forms of cultural capital, which themselves were predicated on hierarchies of the learned vs. the ignorant.[8] The movement of Islamic knowledge circulated in what Michael Lambek has referred to as a "knowledge economy," where scholars were recognized, respected, and followed for their ability to deploy that knowledge appropriately.[9] Knowledge in a Swahili Coast context meant familiarity with the Qur'an, hadith, and *fiqh,* as well as with Kiswahili poetry and proverbs. Randall Pouwels notes that the importance of certain types of knowledge on the Swahili Coast had grown through the nineteenth century, such as scriptural literacy (in Arabic), international travel and contact with other Muslims, Sufi rituals, and—on the economic side—mastery of techniques in the new colonial capitalist economy.[10]

If Kiswahili and Arabic were the local languages of Mombasa's patrician elite, then *kafa'ah* was its mechanism of social reproduction. *Kafa'ah* in an East African context basically describes a gendered mechanism of regulating marriage so that women could only marry a social equal, while men—especially Arab men—could incorporate less prestigious groups

[7] See also B. G. Martin, "Notes on Some Members of the Learned Classes of Zanzibar and East Africa in the Nineteenth Century," *African Historical Studies* 4, no. 3 (1971): 525–45, 529.

[8] Messick, *The Calligraphic State,* 251. Messick refers to how a state produced these hierarchies, but it is important to point out that all that is really needed is a scholarly class. See also Kai Kresse, "Muslim Politics in Postcolonial Kenya: Negotiating Knowledge on the Double-Periphery," *Journal of the Royal Anthropological Institute,* special issue on "Islam, Politics and Anthropology," 15, no. 1 (2009): 76–94.

[9] The phrase is from Michael Lambek, "Certain Knowledge, Contestable Authority: Power and Practice on the Islamic Periphery," *American Ethnologist* 17, no. 1 (1990): 23–40.

[10] Randall Pouwels, "Sh. al-Amin B. Ali Mazrui and Islamic Modernism in East Africa, 1875–1947," *International Journal of Middle East Studies* 13, no. 3 (August 1981): 329–45, 332; Anne Bang, "Islamic Reform in East Africa, ca. 1870–1925: The Alawi Case," paper presented to the workshop "Reasserting Connections, Commonalities, and Cosmopolitanism: The Western Indian Ocean Since 1800," Yale University, November 3–5, 2000, 1–32. Available online at http://www.smi.uib.no/ab/Yale.pdf. Bang calls this part of a more general "enlargement of scale" occurring throughout the region. She makes clear that Islamic modernism was by no means the only set of traveling ideas in this period; Sufi reformist discourse from the Hadhramaut also played a key role.

into their social networks using the mechanism of patrilineal descent.[11] It was through intermarriage that early Arab migrants became Swahili patricians, slaves became wives, and their children became free. Local wives from among the Swahili and Mijikenda often taught the children of their Arab husbands the language and culture of coastal society. *Kafa'ah* preserved Arab genealogy while keeping porous the boundaries of hierarchy and belonging. This principle of intermarriage is in fact the basis for Islamic cosmopolitanism in the Indian Ocean. The challenges to its validity and reproduction throughout the Indian Ocean in the first three decades of the twentieth century—what Enseng Ho calls "the debasement of Arab coin"—were crucial to shaping new imaginings of Arab and Muslim community in Mombasa, Kenya.[12]

Mombasa was a Swahili urban center with a long history in the Indo-African world. The Omanis, the Portuguese, the Ottomans, and various local Swahili groups had all ruled it at various times before the nineteenth century. Two prominent Omani clans—the Busaidi and the Mazrui—fought for control of the city throughout the nineteenth century, with the Busaidis eventually prevailing under Sultan Said bin Sultan. The establishment of the Busaidi capital in Zanzibar in 1840, its consolidation of rule on the mainland coast, and the rise of Omani economic supremacy through trade and plantation agriculture had important implications for the hierarchies of Swahili social stratification. The new Omani settlers may have been initially regarded as upstart newcomers, but their cultural influence subtly shifted the cultural values of the coast toward the values of this new economic elite.[13] These new migrants attained administrative positions in the Busaidi state and made their fortunes off of the booming clove market. In Mombasa, the transition to Busaidi rule meant that Mombasa too profited from the resurgence of Zanzibar commercialism, even as the Busaidi regime repeatedly attempted to undermine Mazrui rule and influence.[14]

---

[11] Enseng Ho, *Graves of Tarim: Genealogy and Mobility Across the Indian Ocean* (Berkeley: University of California Press, 2006), 172. See also Abdul Hamid M. Zein, *The Sacred Meadows: A Structural Analysis of Religious Symbolism in an East African Town* (Evanston, Ill.: Northwestern University Press, 1974), 100.

[12] Ho, *Graves of Tarim,* 174–76, 182–84.

[13] Glassman, *Feasts and Riot,* 33.

[14] Pouwels, "Sh. al-Amin B. Ali Mazrui and Islamic Modernism," 334. Pouwels suggests that Mazrui's polemics against *beni ngoma* and Sufism were influenced by Busaidi support for the *qadi*-ship of Mwinyi Abudi, a popular and well-established Swahili scholar who permitted these practices.

By the 1870s, Mombasa, Malindi, and their surrounding environs had become important grain exporters integrated into a thriving Zanzibari commercial system.[15] But a number of factors undermined the material and social basis for Busaidi and Mazrui supremacy in the late nineteenth century. In 1885, the Imperial British East Africa Company (IBEAC) "leased" a ten-mile strip of coastline from the sultan of Zanzibar and later intervened to install a compliant *liwali* (local administrator) in the coastal Mazrui stronghold of Takaungu.[16] As the British Foreign Office gradually undermined the sovereignty of Zanzibar's sultans, British interests also acted to prevent Germany from gaining control over the Kenya coast. In 1896, Great Britain formally declared a protectorate over British holdings on the eastern coast of Africa and assumed control of IBEAC lands. The intervention of the British is the temporal starting point of my historical explanation of *al-Islah*'s discourse; the establishment of colonial rule is significant for how it helped shape the discourse of *al-Islah*'s founder and first editor, Sheikh al-Amin Mazrui.

Al-Amin was born in 1891 in Kibokoni, in Old Town Mombasa, and raised by his uncle, Sheikh Suleiman Mazrui, the chief *qadi* of Kenya.[17] While he was primarily educated in Mombasa and Zanzibar, Sheikh al-Amin was also influenced by the discursive currents of Islamic reform sweeping throughout the Indian Ocean in the early twentieth century.[18] The work of Muhammad Abduh and Rashid Rida encouraged Sheikh al-Amin in his calls for the reform of Mombasa's urban space; he rooted his local vision of Mombasa in their transnational vision of Islamic unity with

---

[15] Fred Cooper, *From Slaves to Squatters: Plantation Labor and Agriculture in Zanzibar and Coastal Kenya* (Portsmouth, N.H.: Heinemann, 1997), 110; Richard E. Stren, *Housing the Urban Poor in Africa: Policy, Politics, and Bureaucracy in Mombasa* (Berkeley: University of California Press, Institute of International Studies, 1977), 8; Justin Willis, *Mombasa, Swahili and the Making of Mijikenda* (Oxford: Clarendon, 1993), 64.

[16] Tim Carmichael, "British 'Practice' Towards Islam in the East Africa Protectorate: Muslim Officials, Waqf Administration, and Secular Education in Mombasa and Environs, 1895–1920," *Journal of Muslim Minority Affairs* 17, no. 2 (1997): 296. The IBEAC originally secured its claim by signing a treaty with the Mazrui, who claimed to sign on behalf of the Mijikenda. Willis, *Making of Mijikenda,* 128.

[17] For more on the biography of Sheikh al-Amin, see Ghalib Yusuf Tamim, *Maisha ya Sheikh al-Amin bin Ali Mazrui (1891–1947)* (Nairobi: Signal, 2005). I am indebted to Prof. Ali Mazrui for this source.

[18] Al-Amin's education included study under two leading Sufi sheikhs from the Hadhramaut—Abdul Bin Sumayt and Abdallah Bakathir. See Bang, "Islamic Reform in East Africa."

the Arabic language as its passport.[19] Sheikh al-Amin emphasized Arabic literacy, a modernized Islamic education, and a focus on the legacy of pious ancestors. In Mombasa, these ancestors (*wazee*) were Arabs with a local genealogy stretching back as far as the first settlements by Arabs in East Africa. In the political context of urban Mombasa, Sheikh al-Amin believed Arabs had a special role to play in educating other local Muslims, and he himself led several efforts in the educational sphere.[20]

Sheikh al-Amin was by no means the first East African intellectual to be influenced by Rida and Abduh,[21] but he was the first to propagate their ideas of Islamic modernism outside of elite, scholarly networks in a language (Kiswahili) that was more broadly understood by all coastal Muslims. As a teacher, public lecturer, and journalist, he was at the forefront in advocating for educational and social reform among Muslims, and was active in propagating these ideas through *al-Islah* as well as pamphlets and sermons.[22] *Al-Islah* brought the "knowledge currency" of elite texts and ideas outside of the genealogical networks of traditional Islamic knowledge and into broad circulation, thus opening up new avenues for inculcating piety and creating virtuous subjects. Advances in print technology worked with the idea of a transnational Muslim community to make conformity in Islamic belief and practice something possible for ulama like Sheikh al-Amin to "imagine" more explicitly than ever before. It also made the existence of localized custom more visibly threatening to

[19] Similar intellectual currents were sweeping Zanzibar at this time. See Amal Ghazal, *Islamic Reform and Arab Nationalism: Expanding the Crescent from the Mediterranean to the Indian Ocean (1880s–1930s)* (New York: Routledge, 2010), 100; Ho, *Graves of Tarim,* 157, 182. See also Anne K. Bang, "Cosmopolitanism Colonized? Three Cases from Zanzibar 1890–1925," in *Struggling with History,* ed. Kresse and Simpson, 172.

[20] Roman Loimeier, *Between Social Skills and Marketable Skills: The Politics of Islamic Education in 20th Century Zanzibar* (Leiden: Brill, 2009), 110.

[21] One early example of an East African *ʿalim* influenced by the ideas of *al-Manar* and other Islamic newspapers from the wider Arab world was Sayyid Mansab b. Ali. See Abdallah S. Farsy, *The Shafiʾi Ulama of East Africa, c. 1830–1970: A Hagiographic Account,* trans., ed., and anno. Randall L. Pouwels (Madison: University of Wisconsin Program of African Studies, 1989), 22–26.

[22] Pouwels, "Sh. al-Amin B. Ali Mazrui and Islamic Modernism," 332. See also F. H. Elmasri, "Sheikh al-Amin bin Ali al-Mazrui and the Islamic Intellectual Tradition in East Africa," *Journal of Muslim Minority Affairs* 8, no. 2 (July 1987): 199–237. For more on the history of the Mazruis in East Africa, see Ibrahim E. Soghayroun, "The Arab and Swahili Culture in Historical Perspective: Some Important Links in 'The History of the Mazrūʿīs in East Africa' by Shaykh al-Amīn b. ʿAlī al-Mazrūʿī," *Sudanic Africa* 12 (2001): 16.

the foundation of Muslim society in East Africa. I argue that the ideas of reform and purification contributed strongly to later Arab-led nationalist movements on the East African coast.

Again and again in his writings, al-Amin chastised Swahili and Arab townspeople for their idleness and ignorance. He strongly critiqued certain traditional practices of the Swahili town elite (*ngoma, maulidi, dhikri,* visiting *waganga*), which were also shared by neighboring Mijikenda communities. He imagined a local Muslim community led by Arabs and purified of these elements of local coastal culture.[23] His critiques also singled out recent Muslim converts of Mijikenda and up-country origins. Sheikh al-Amin's thinking was acutely oriented toward a vision of the urban space of Mombasa as a pious, orderly Muslim space governed by the legal and social supremacy of the shariʾa. The social interaction among the Arab and Swahili elite in the coastal towns was a space in which Sheikh al-Amin's critiques might resonate.[24]

On February 29, 1932, the first issue of *al-Islah* came off the presses, and the paper's concerns reflected the local issues of this elite. *Al-Islah* recorded events like the building of new mosques, the formation of Islamic welfare organizations, and the appointment of new *qadis* (Islamic judges). It also offered its readers a section on international news, where they learned about Muslims in Europe, the struggles of a newly independent Iraq, and other pressing world issues affecting Muslims. There were sections that routinely discussed the "progress of Muslims" in which the authors emphasized cultural issues of Arabic linguistic competence, implementation of shariʾa, and the ideal Muslim woman. Finally, there were letters to the editor in which we can see readers not merely absorbing the news, lessons, and ideas of the newspaper, but wrestling with and reshaping them, probing further into *al-Islah*'s provocative editorials.

From the perspective of Sheikh al-Amin, the religion, language, and identity of East African Arabs were under attack. As we saw, in Sheikh

---

[23] See, for example, the tradition of Siku ya Mwaka in Zein, *The Sacred Meadows,* chapter 7. For a history of *maulidi* in Kenya and a sense of the current debates over its performance, see Kai Kresse, "Debating Maulidi: Ambiguities and Transformations of Muslim Identity Along the Kenyan Swahili Coast," in *The Global Worlds of the Swahili,* ed. R. Loimeier and R. Seesemann (Berlin: LIT-Verlag, 2006), 211–30.

[24] Pouwels, "Sh. al-Amin B. Ali Mazrui and Islamic Modernism," 334; Lambek, "Foreword," xvii.

al-Amin's own lifetime, the prestige of the town's Arab elite was severely undermined and the habitus of its inhabitants shifted loose from its Arab-Islamic cultural moorings. In order to continue being good Muslims, Mombasa's Arabs—especially its youth—would have to be instructed on their proper role within the community. Other Muslim residents of the town (Swahili and Mijikenda) had similar obligations to learn how to enact their proper social and religious roles. Through *al-Islah,* Sheikh al-Amin sought to imagine a community based on the Islamic ideal of the equality of every believer, but predicated that equality on the local ideal of leaving behind *ushenzi* and coming into knowledge, beginning with knowledge of shariʾa.[25]

According to Sheikh al-Amin, ignorant people could not rule knowledgeable ones. The ignorant people were the British who, although powerful, did not understand the historical role of shariʾa in building Islamic community, and the *Watu wa Afrika* whose *ujinga* (ignorance) led them to follow the British in adopting native customary law instead of shariʾa. *Al-Islah* chastised those who *should* be the most knowledgeable (the Arab elite, especially, but also the Swahili) as betraying their duty to lead society by refusing to be guided by the knowledgeable among them and by being satisfied with an indolent and unproductive lifestyle.[26] If even the putative leaders of the coastal Muslim community—those acquainted with Islam over many centuries—could not read and write Arabic, how could the community reproduce itself and instruct its youth on proper moral comportment? Indeed, warned Sheikh al-Amin, the ignorance of the Muslims was dangerous because, at the same time that they were falling behind, up-country people were seizing knowledge of their own, knowledge not dependent on their integration into established Islamic networks. "We will be the ones sold into slavery if it returns," warned Sheikh al-Amin.[27]

As we saw above, the British took over administration of the Kenyan coast from IBEAC in 1897. Initially, the new colonial administration moved circumspectly, avoiding open confrontation with the Arab elite

---

[25] See, for example, "Haja Yetu Kubwa: Madrasa ya Jumʾiyatul-Islamiyah na Wajibu Wetu kwa Tarafu Yake," *Al-Islah,* September 12, 1932, where Sheikh al-Amin emphasizes the importance of studying Arabic, the *ilm* (knowledge) of Islam, and the "biographies of our elders."

[26] "Kukataa kuongozwa ni ujinga ya pili," *al-Islah,* October 17, 1932.

[27] Quoted in Pouwels, "Sh. al-Amin B. Ali Mazrui and Islamic Modernism," 340.

and ruling through the Zanzibar sultan's Arab administrators—the *liwali*, the *qadi*, and the *mudir*.[28] The British representative in Zanzibar, Arthur Hardinge, paid lip service to a continuity of administration in East Africa in which shariʾa would still be enforced by local experts. Generally, British reforms initially allowed for Arab officials to be given administrative positions and to judge civil and criminal cases on the coast, or to advise European judges who would administer Islamic law in "Native Courts" under the provisions of the Indian Penal Code.[29] In 1897, a chief *qadi* position was even created, the Shaykh al-Islam, along with a dual legal system administered by a High Court in Zanzibar.[30] But these reforms, while appearing to give prestige to Islamic law courts, actually undermined the diversity and flexibility of the shariʾa as it was constituted under the prestige of individual *qadis*.[31] Furthermore, British attempts to create and codify an Islamic law code "were an eclectic patchwork of provisions taken from various schools of Islamic law" and thus in violation of loyalties to certain schools of law within the Islamic tradition.[32] In this system, Muslims were recognized as a homogenous legal community to be governed by shariʾa. The British acted as if the shariʾa was one more type of customary law, to be codified rationally and administered in cooperation with local authorities.

Drastic changes followed the completion of the Uganda railway in 1901. The railway enabled new mobility for up-country migrants who came as contract laborers and spurred regular traffic between Mombasa and its western hinterlands. In 1904, the British shifted their administration away from the coast to Nairobi and established separate consular representatives for British East Africa and Zanzibar.[33] In 1907, slavery was

[28] The role of the head or "coast" *liwali* was roughly equivalent to the role of the provincial commissioner, the role of district *liwali* to that of the district commissioner, and the role of the *mudir* to that of the district officer. The *qadis* had independent jurisdiction. Stren, *Housing the Urban Poor in Africa,* 10.

[29] A code which was, as indicated, borrowed from the British colonial administration in India.

[30] Carmichael, "British 'Practice' Towards Islam," 297. See also Randall Pouwels, *Horn and Crescent: Cultural Change and Traditional Islam on the East African Coast, 800–1900* (Cambridge, Eng.: Cambridge University Press, 1987), 174–77.

[31] Bang, "Cosmpolitanism Colonized?" 177.

[32] Pouwels, *Horn and Crescent,* 177. See also S. S. Abrahams, "The Reorganization of the Zanzibar Courts," *Journal of Comparative Legislation and International Law,* Third Series, 6, no. 4 (1924): 293–300.

[33] Pouwels, *Horn and Crescent,* 166.

abolished in the Protectorate, striking at the productive heart of plantation agriculture and forcing former slaves and former masters to renegotiate their relationship in terms of squatting, clientage, and tenancy.[34] The destruction of the plantation agricultural system based on slave labor, which had contributed to Mombasa's florescence under the Busaidis and enriched many of the town's patricians, only aggravated the sense that their destiny was no longer in their hands. And the announcement of abolition forced the British into a confrontation over the marriages of ex-slaves, which many *qadis* refused to sanction without the consent of the slave's former master. When the British intervened in disputes like these (which had important implications for inheritance), they explicitly placed shariʾa on the level with "Native law" (customary law) and limited its application to criminal and civil cases "in which Mohamedans are parties."[35] British interventions into the realm of shariʾa—both its attempts to uphold it and its attempts to limit its influence—were, as we shall see, a major grievance of Sheikh al-Amin and *al-Islah*'s readers.

Further damage to the social and economic prestige of the Arab elite followed. In 1908, the Land Titles Ordinance passed, and the British claimed all "waste" land as Crown Land and began to consider "native" claims to land rights, over which many Swahili and Arab patricians claimed title. Between 1910 and 1912, Arabs were exempted from the hut tax, which would seem to have been an enormous benefit to them, but which began to create an administrative divide between them and the often-indistinguishable Swahili.[36] By 1921, Arabs were ambiguously classified as "natives" under criminal law and "non-natives" for taxation purposes.[37] Initially, a native was defined as a person born in Africa who was not of European or Asiatic origin, but people of mixed race—like many Arabs and Swahili—continually stymied British attempts to "see" the true and natural identity of their colonial subjects. This ambiguous status provoked protest, uneasiness, and defiant letters to the editor of *al-Islah,* signed "*Mzalia wa Africa*" (native of Africa) or "*Mzalia wa Unguja*" (native of Zanzibar).

---

[34] Cooper, *From Slaves to Squatters,* 82–83.

[35] Minute Paper 84, Provincial Commissioner Seyyiddie, 1912.

[36] Margaret Strobel, *Muslim Women in Mombasa, 1890–1975* (New Haven, Conn.: Yale University Press, 1979), 39, 74.

[37] A. I. Salim, *The Swahili-Speaking Peoples of Kenya's Coast, 1895–1965* (Nairobi: East African Publishing House, 1973), 188.

The depression of the 1920s and 1930s, which afflicted much of the coast, did not affect Mombasa in the same way. While Takaungu, Malindi, Mambrui, Lamu, and other cities lost population, Mombasa's continued to increase. From 1900 to 1970, Mombasa's population went from 25,000 to 250,000.[38] By 1917, the population had increased to 31,000 on Mombasa Island alone; the district contained over 44,000 residents. By 1932, the year *al-Islah* began publishing, the population of Mombasa District (including the urban areas around Mombasa Island) had ballooned to 54,894. These population registers did not always count the "floating element" of up-country laborers who remained on the coast only seasonally.[39] Nevertheless, they amply demonstrate the demographic changes that were engulfing the city.

New economic conditions fueled this population increase. In 1921, a new deepwater port was constructed on the eastern side of Mombasa Island at Kilindi, with two deepwater berths constructed there five years later.[40] A modern business district grew up around this new port, removing the elite neighborhood of Old Town from the center of Mombasa's economic life. This new construction, combined with the intensification of railway service to the colonial capital in Nairobi, brought an enormous influx of labor, not only of "up-country" Kikuyu and Luo, but Mijikenda from the rural areas surrounding Mombasa.[41] Up-country people largely became seasonal laborers or worked for the colonial administration, oftentimes as local police officers (*askari*), while Mijikenda took jobs as "casual laborers" on the dock.[42] By the early 1920s, the Mijikenda were

[38] Strobel, *Muslim Women in Mombasa,* 7.

[39] Karim Janmohamed, "A History of Mombasa c. 1895–1939: Some Aspects of Economic and Social Life in an East African Port Town During Colonial Rule" (Ph.D. diss., Northwestern University, 1978), 251–57. See also Sara Mirza and Margaret Strobel, eds. and trans., *Three Swahili Women: Life Histories from Mombasa, Kenya* (Bloomington: Indiana University Press, 1989). They give Mombasa's population as 25,000 in 1900 and 100,000 in 1950.

[40] Fred Cooper, *On the African Waterfront: Urban Disorder and the Transformation of Work in Colonial Mombasa* (New Haven, Conn.: Yale University Press, 1987), 27. Joseph Samuel Caruso, "Politics in Colonial Kenya, 1929–1963: A History of Kilifi District" (Ph.D. diss., Columbia University, 1993), 140; Stren, *Housing the Urban Poor in Africa,* 14; Willis, *Making of Mijikenda,* 148.

[41] The Mijikenda (also known in the literature as the WaNyika) refer to approximately 12–15 groups speaking mutually intelligible languages and inhabiting the coastal hinterlands (*Nyika*).

[42] Annual Report, Mombasa District, 1911–1912.

a dominant demographic in many parts of the coast and served as key members of the casual labor force.[43] Frederick Cooper shows that these various labor populations brought with them their own labor patterns and communal identities.[44] These labor migrations birthed a new kind of labor militancy and provoked a cultural and political reaction from more long-standing urban residents like elite Arabs.[45]

The British and the patrician elite were united in their uneasiness about the existence of this new floating population. Many of these migrants to Mombasa were not Muslims at all and had little interest in Islam or the *uungwana* and *uustaraabu* ideals of the urban elite. British administrators in the coastal towns frequently warned of the dangers of a non-Muslim colonial police force made up of up-country people. In 1926, the *Mombasa Times* called for the detaining and checking of the certificates of casual laborers, and there was a 1932 effort to expel unemployed "vagrants" from the city.[46] But, since Mombasa was considered a "native town," British attempts at legislating this perceived disorder were minimal and many evaded their attempts. Mijikenda and other new migrants moved through a Mombasa poised between its cosmopolitan Islamic past and its equally cosmopolitan colonial capitalist future. The plurality of their strategies and the response of Sheikh al-Amin and the readers of *al-Islah* is the subject of the next section.

Shariʾa, Colonialism, and the Mijikenda

Part of what British colonialism had done, in the view of Sheikh al-Amin, was to break the association between Islamic knowledge and social

---

[43] Caruso, "Politics in Colonial Kenya," 13; Stren, *Housing the Urban Poor in Africa,* 18.

[44] Cooper, *On the African Waterfront,* 28.

[45] Karim Janmohamed, "Ethnicity in an Urban Setting: A Case Study of Mombasa," in *Hadith 6: History and Social Change in East Africa,* ed. B. A. Ogot (Nairobi: East African Literature Bureau, 1976), 201. The tension between up-country migrants and "Shihiri" Arab laborers from Hadhramaut took a violent turn in the 1937 riots between Luo and Hadhrami, where fourteen Arabs and one Luo were killed. Similar riots involving Hadhramis and also poor Omani migrants (Wamanga) occurred in Zanzibar as early as 1928. The strikes and other conflicts like rioting alerted the British to the "dangers" of up-country labor and the need for an "orderly" working class.

[46] As early as 1915 the British passed the Native Registration Ordinance, requiring adult males to register with the government and carry a pass known as a *kipande.* See Willis, *Making of Mijikenda,* 198–99; Janmohamed, "A History of Mombasa," 406–8.

prestige, causing people to forget their obligations within the knowledge economy. Knowledgeable people shared what they knew with others, while those without knowledge sought to gain more and followed those who had it. In colonial Mombasa, however, the hierarchies were reversed. The Arabs—those who should have been most knowledgeable, according to Sheikh al-Amin—were mired in ignorance of their language and fruitless attempts to imitate the culture and education of the colonialists.[47] The *washenzi,* including recent Muslim converts among them, were clinging to the authority of their own kinds of (in his view) manifestly inferior knowledge (like tribal custom) or claiming to authoritatively interpret the knowledge bases of coastal Islam without sufficient learning. In particular, Sheikh al-Amin singled out the Digo, a group of Mijikenda who lived adjacent to Mombasa. The Digo and other Mijikenda had a long and rich history of association with Mombasa.[48] The Mazrui family, rulers of Mombasa for much of the eighteenth and nineteenth centuries, cultivated a close relationship with these neighboring Mijikenda.[49]

Both Arab and Swahili sheikhs had acted as patrons of the Mijikenda and arbitrated their disputes; the Mijikenda, for their part, had defended the town on numerous occasions and had once helped to restore the Mazrui to power after Busaidi agents had assassinated the Mazrui *liwali.*[50] Many of the Swahili elite's cultural traditions—ritual healing, dance patterns, and yearly celebrations—shared much in common with Mijikenda culture. There was a great degree of intermarriage between Mijikenda women and Swahili *waungwana* men, especially in areas where the two were neighbors.[51]

In the nineteenth and early twentieth centuries, Mijikenda migrants were able to "become" Swahili and integrate themselves more or less as

---

[47] Al-Amin bin Aly, "Namna Gani Twaigiza Wazungu," in *Uwongozi* (Mombasa: East African Muslim Welfare Society, 1955), 6–8.

[48] Willis, *Making of Mijikenda,* 104. For a detailed treatment of the Islamization of the Mijikenda (the Giriama, Digo, Duruma, Chonyi, Kambe, Ribe, Jibana, Kauma, and Rabai), see David C. Sperling, "The Growth of Islam Among the Mijikenda of the Kenyan Coast, 1826–1933" (Ph.D. diss., University of London, 1988).

[49] Thomas Spear, *The Kaya Complex: A History of the Mijikenda Peoples of the Kenya Coast to 1900* (Nairobi: Kenya Literature Bureau, 1978), 134–35.

[50] F. J. Berg, "Mombasa Under the Busaidi Sultanate: The City and Its Hinterlands in the Nineteenth Century" (Ph.D. diss., University of Wisconsin, 1971), 46.

[51] Berg, "Mombasa Under the Busaidi Sultanate," 89, 166. See also Mirza and Strobel, *Three Swahili Women,* 8, 45–46.

townspeople. This very integration, because of migrants' continued links to their home areas, steadily undermined the social distinction between them and the *waungwana.*[52] This thick network of overlapping social identities was inimicable to separate spheres of colonial administration. British rule focused on administratively separating Mombasa District from its predominantly Mijikenda hinterlands, expelling Swahili and Arab traders from Mijikenda reserves and encouraging the Mijikenda to "remember" their "native customs" and rule according to "native law."[53] Thus, the British impulse to make the cosmopolitan social space of the towns more legible and to distinguish absolutely between Muslim and non-Muslim legal spheres threw into disarray the networks of marriage, trade, and religion linking coastal Swahili, Arab, and Mijikenda.[54]

In 1913, the provincial commissioner for the Coast (Seyyidie) Province, C. W. Hobley, gave an explicit policy recommendation through a letter that illuminates how the British sought to keep up the appearance of respect for Islam while severely curtailing its influence.

> I desire it however, to be clearly understood that administrative officers are not in any way to depart from the path of strict neutrality with regards to Islamism: the information contained in the letter, viz. "that the late Kathi [*sic*] of Wassin did his utmost although without success to persuade the Kubo (hereditary chief) of the Wa Digo to relinquish Wa Digo tribal laws and customs" is to my mind a definite case in which a Government official is using his official position to spread his religion . . . any attempt on their part [Arab admin.] to influence the tribes near the coast be they Digo, Duruma, Kamba &c. to embrace Mohamedanism or to relinquish their land laws and legitimate customs for the sheria will be reported to the Government . . .

He then states that he favors the idea that the Digo and other Nyika tribes should be separated from Arab (Islamic) influence and encouraged to rule in their tribunals according to their particular tribal law.[55] The

[52] Janmohamed, "Ethnicity in an Urban Setting," 194–95.
[53] Willis, *Making of Mijikenda,* 64. British policy was in many ways a carryover of the German missionary Johann Ludwig Krapf's fear that coastal Muslims in the hinterland would exert a disproportionate influence on the Mijikenda.
[54] Willis, *Making of Mijikenda,* 52.
[55] Kilifi District Political Record Book, vol. I. PRB 110/Kfi/11, reel 72.

boundaries of shariʾa's application, in Hobley's thinking, were only those "definite communities of Swahilis, Arabs or other people who have become permanently detribalized or to coin a word, Swahilized."[56] The aim of British policy was not only to isolate the Mijikenda from what the British viewed as the undue legal influence of shariʾa, but also to intervene to "seal the permeable boundaries of ethnicity" by which Mijikenda had become Muslim Swahili.[57] The British attempted to create a wall of separation between the Mijikenda and the coastal Muslim townsmen. They pontificated against the presence of coastal traders (often Shihiri Arabs from Hadramaut or Muslim Indians) in Mijikenda reserves and speculated that the Wadigo would be contaminated and adopt the "slothful inertia of the Mohammedan" due to close contact with coastal residents.[58]

By linking ethnic identity to separate legal spheres, the British undermined the recognized hegemony of shariʾa in a plurality of legal fields under colonialism. One district commissioner even obtained decisions from some Digo that they would rather be governed by customary law than by shariʾa.[59] Individual Digo were encouraged by British attitudes and took advantage of the legal pluralism of the colonial law systems to obtain advantageous legal decisions; in 1915, several Muslim Digo government headmen claimed property from inheritance under matrilineal customary law after their claims were not upheld in the *qadi* court. This pluralism extended to other spheres outside of law and to other groups of Mijikenda. Many Giriama, for example, had converted to Islam, yet continued to sit on clan councils with other non-Muslim Mijikenda elders; others who did not convert nevertheless adopted certain ritual symbols of Islamic identity and practiced ritual healing through Islamic idioms.[60]

---

[56] Kilifi District Political Record Book, reel 72.

[57] Willis, *Making of Mijikenda,* 73, 116.

[58] Annual Report, Takaungu Sub-District 1915–1916, 2423/AR in 22/177, reel 59.

[59] 2426/AR/1915-16. Part of the British motivation behind the 1908 Land Ordinances Law was a paternalistic desire to "protect" the Mijikenda from the land claims of the Arabs and Swahili, because the Mijikenda, in the British view, thought only in terms of "communal land." Ironically, British policy actually set in motion the very thing they were trying to prevent—the sale of Mijikenda land to Swahili and Arabs. See Willis, *Making of Mijikenda,* 123–27.

[60] David Parkin, *Palms, Wine and Witnesses: Public Spirit and Private Gain in an African Farming Community* (San Francisco: Chandler, 1972), 40–43. Parkin calls these people "therapeutic Muslims" and their practice "ritual syncretism." See David Parkin, "The Politics of Ritual Syncretism," *Africa* 40 (1970): 217–33. For a ritual on Mafia Island off the coast of Tanzania, involving both Islamic symbols (*dhikr* and Arabic) and non-Islamic ones

The British also endeavored to set up Mijikenda elders in "Native Councils" (*Ngambi*), which were empowered to give legal rulings based on Nyika "customary law." So, while there were Muslim *qadis* overseeing cases at Mambrui, Malindi, Takaungu, Mombasa, and Wasin (with the chief *qadi* at Mombasa) in 1912, there were also parallel groups of *Ngambi* operating among the Digo, the Duruma, the Giriama, and other Mijikenda groups that were ruled by British-appointed "Presidents of Councils."[61] In the Annual Report of 1912 from Mombasa District, the district commissioner proposed, "The mudirs courts might with advantage be placed in the same category as the native tribunals under which they could exercise jurisdiction only over Mohamedan natives and an appeal from them would be to the District Commissioner, by this means the mudirs would form part of the Administrative staff of the District instead of an independent judiciary."[62]

As early as 1915, the *Wangambi* were being encouraged by the British to adopt a more autonomous stance and to rule according to customary law, whereas they had originally "only existed as an informal arbitration board to represent matters to the *liwali* (Muslim administrator) and had no powers in itself."[63] By 1924, these *Ngambi* were established throughout most African rural areas in the Colony and Protectorate.[64] Several attempts at instituting a *Ngambi* within Mombasa and other coastal urban centers failed, but the British tried again in 1932 to institute the *Ngambi* within Mombasa District.[65] Meanwhile, they continued struggling to bring a logical order to the way legal spheres were defined along ethnic lines.[66]

(the drinking of blood), see Ann Patricia Caplan, *Choice and Constraint in a Swahili Community: Property, Hierarchy, and Cognatic Descent on the East African Coast* (London: Oxford University Press for the International African Institute, 1975), 119.

[61] Annual Report, Malindi District, 1911–1912. In Mombasa the town magistrate exercised authority throughout the district and there were *mudir* courts in the surrounding area.

[62] Annual Report, Mombasa District, 1912–1913, 2413/AR in 8/157, reel 59.

[63] Annual Report, Mombasa District, 1915–1916, 2426/AR/1915-16, reel 60.

[64] Stren, *Housing the Urban Poor in Africa,* 42.

[65] Native Affairs Report Annual Report, 1932, 2528/AR/1413, reel 62.

[66] "Appellate Civil Court, The Public Trustee of the Colony and Protectorate of Kenya as Trustee of the Estate of Ali bin Abdulkarim v. Jiwa bin Bwana Hindi Ganeji," in Court of Appeal for Eastern Africa, *Law Reports Containing Decisions of the Court of Appeal for Eastern Africa,* vol. 1 (1934) (Nairobi: Government Printer, 1934), 117–18. Three years later, another decision involving inheritance before the Court of Appeals for Eastern Africa engaged in similar slippage, expressing difficulty in thinking of the law of Islam as "native law," "merely because it is the law applicable to many, or even all, of the natives of the

In a 1927 case before the Court of Appeal for Eastern Africa, the judges considered an inheritance case of a "member of the WaDigo tribe who was a Mohammedan." The original Native Council (*Ngambi*) had decided in favor of matrilineal descent by WaDigo custom; this decision had been upheld by a British Second Class District Court at Kwale but overturned by the Supreme Court of Kenya, who ruled that "where natives are Mahommedans the Mahommedan law, in my opinion, applies to them." The Court of Appeals upheld the Supreme Court's decision, adding that since the WaDigo "are a tribe and not a sect," the special proviso according special sects of Islam their own inheritance rules did not apply.[67] Thus, the context of Sheikh al-Amin's writings in the early 1930s is that of the prospect of a further decline in importance of shariʾa and the erosion of its prestige as a socio-legal system.

Reconstituting the Role of Knowledge: Sheikh al-Amin's Vision of Community

Sheikh al-Amin creatively addressed the alleged failures of the Digo to take on their responsibilities as Muslims in an article entitled "Katika Ndia ya ulingano wa Mwenyezi Mungu" ("The Way of Harmony with God").[68] His narrative linked the arrival of Islam in the East Africa community and the Salafi tradition of pious ancestors with those Arabs who had first set foot on East African shores: "Our elders (*wazee wetu*) supervised spreading Islam in every part of Africa where they arrived . . . they transformed the people of this town [Mombasa] in a short time and expelled *ushenzi* and caused the culture of their town to change to one of worshipping God alone." Sheikh al-Amin's imagined community drew on an original event in which a civilized community, rooted in the shariʾa, was established in Mombasa by righteous and knowledgeable people.

Despite their efforts, al-Amin wrote, the elders failed to repair the character (*tabia*) of those who entered Islam, even through education in the

Kenya Protectorate." See "Khamis bin Ahmed v. Ahmed bin ali bin Abdurehman and eight others," in C.A. 16/1934, *Law Reports Containing Decisions of the Court of Appeal for Eastern Africa,* 130–33.

[67] C.A. 27/1927 in Kenya Supreme Court, *Law reports of Kenya containing cases determined by the Supreme Court of the Colony and Protectorate of Kenya* (Nairobi: Kenya Colony and Protectorate, 1953), vol. 14, 30–32.

[68] "Katika Ndia ya ulingano wa Mwenyezi Mungu," *al-Islah,* April 11, 1932.

shariʾa, because many of these new Muslims didn't know how to pray, let alone comprehend the other responsibilities of their new religion. "Many still hold onto their *ushenzi* customs and their incorrect beliefs. And if we don't succeed in following our elders—who had taught these people shariʾa and instructed them well and forbade them from evil and improved their character—then the work of our elders and the effort they made will be worthlessly lost."[69]

In "Katika," memory of the role of Arabs in Islamicizing Mombasa and other coastal areas was called upon to give moral force to the work of communal unity and moral rearmament of Mombasa's urban space. "It's very upsetting," wrote Sheikh al-Amin, "that many of our neighbors do not know a thing about their religion and this is what has caused them to become hardened in their customs of marriage and inheritance. And if they knew their religion they would leave these 'bitter' customs and hold to shariʾa like the way they hold to their knowledgeable brothers."[70] Restoring the correct relationships of the rule of knowledge in guiding people out of ignorance would help the Digo to become better Muslims. It would also cause them to leave behind their customary law and follow shariʾa.

But it was not only knowledge at stake in the hegemony of the shariʾa. One might legitimately ask why shariʾa was so important to the patrician elite if they were still able to exercise their right for their cases to be heard in front of a *qadi.* One possible answer is that erosion of the shariʾa struck directly at the basis for the social reproduction of the town's elite. As we saw in the introduction, it was common practice for Swahili and Arab Muslim townsmen to take wives from among the non-Muslim population. In the pre-colonial era, this was a route to social prestige for the wife and her family. *Kafaʾah* was the glue cementing the bonds of social reproduction; it made possible a socially unified population out of the diversity of urban life and reproduced a patrilineal cosmopolitan genealogy based on a recognized hierarchy—a path through which diverse populations could be civilized by being brought out of *ushenzi* and into *ungwana* or *ustaarabu.* Sheikh al-Amin had written about the importance of *kafaʾah* in a treatise on marriage in which he stressed the importance of social equality between husband and wife. According to Shāfiʿī law, a marriage is invalid if a woman is married by her guardian to someone below her social status. *Kafaʾah* impacted the social reputations of both the bride and her guardian;

---

[69] "Katika Ndia ya ulingano wa Mwenyezi Mungu."

[70] Ibid.

flouting its guidelines would lead to social chaos and the collapse of the patrilineal prestige of the family unit.[71]

But *al-Islah*'s readers also understood that *kafa'ah* had implications for colonial debates about citizenship and belonging. *Kafa'ah* was also what helped Arabs lay claim to being indigenous residents of East Africa, and letters to the editor in *al-Islah* show that readers were aware of *kafa'ah*'s importance to social reproduction. After looking in his English-Swahili dictionary for definitions of the word "native," one *al-Islah* reader discovered the following definitions: *mtu wa asli* (indigenous person), *mtu mweusi* (black person), *mshenzi* (barbarian), and *mzalia* (literally: someone born in a place). After studying the meanings for a while, the truth dawned on him: many Arabs were indeed indigenous residents of East Africa and, because of intermarriage, it was impossible to separate them from indigenous Africans. He then critiqued European racial conceptions in which "mixed race" offspring of European and African parents were deemed to be "Coloured" and despised because of it, in contrast to the Arab method of patrilineal intermarriage described earlier.[72] Arab-Islamic *kafa'ah* was thus, to the reader, a manifestly superior way of constituting identity; it had been converting *washenzi* into Arabs since Muhammad's establishment of Islamic rule in Medina 1,351 years earlier, he wrote.[73]

But when customary law became a distinct and equal sphere to that of shari'a, then *kafa'ah* could be overturned and a woman's lineage could gain certain rights over her and her offspring through laws of matrilineal succession, even if she came from a non-Muslim background, thus creating the destabilizing possibility that those born Muslim could be redefined and raised as pagan *washenzi.* In the case of the Mijikenda Digo, we saw how the local *Wangambi* frequently used a mixture of Islamic law and customary law to settle cases; a number of non-Muslim Digo men inherited the wives of their deceased Muslim relatives.

Readers of *al-Islah* were aware of these cases, and they wrote in response to Sheikh al-Amin's numerous critiques of the *Ngambi.* One

[71] Mohamed S. Mraja, "The Reform Ideas of Shaykh ʿAbdallāh Ṣāliḥ al-Farsī and the Transformation of Marital Practices Among Digo Muslims of Kenya," *Islamic Law and Society* 17 (2010): 269.

[72] "Waarabu na Jina la Native Wazungu nao hupawa jina hili wazaliwapo Kenya?" *al-Islah,* October 24, 1932.

[73] "Waarabu na Jina la Native Wazungu."

concerned reader, Ali Roshein, wrote, "The purpose of these *Ngambi* is expressly to remove shariʾa and to lead the Arabs astray." Moving from the general concern over the erosion of shariʾa, Roshein expressed a disbelief about a recent court judgment: "Also I have gotten news of a judgment on a Nyika woman who has been a Muslim now for some time and has married a Muslim man and had children with him. She has been judged by these ignorant *Wangambi* (Native judges) and in their 'wisdom' they judged that this woman should return to the Nyika and that her children should be Wa-Nyika [Mijikenda] . . . the youth of Islam will be caused to pass into unbelief through this pattern."[74]

In light of these trends, Sheikh al-Amin critiqued both customary and British colonial law. While acknowledging that the "*kanuni za Kizungu*" (colonial British law), the "*sharīʾa ya Islamu*" (Islamic law), and the "*Milla ya Watu wa Africa*" (customs of the Africans) had differences not only between them but within them, al-Amin pointed out that the British limited shariʾa to a circumscribed number of issues on marriage, divorce, inheritance, and little else. He contrasted this with the "customs of the blacks," which were used in most cases by the British except in major murder cases and rebellion against the government. "If it [a case] is in the cities and there are no *Ngambi,* it will typically be judged by the British according to British colonial law. But the judge will make an effort to utilize the native custom of the defendant unless the judge sees that British colonial law will give a better judgment than customary law."[75] This method, accused al-Amin, would inevitably bring about a corruption of justice. In his view, British colonial law was both unjust in its verdicts and hypocritical in its application—especially when it made concessions to customary law.[76]

If British law supplanted shariʾa as the hegemonic law code for Muslims and non-Muslims alike, al-Amin argued, shariʾa was doomed to be a narrowly confessional code applied to Muslims in the same manner that customary law was applied to different ethnic groups. Al-Amin also linked

---

[74] Baruwa Wasomaji, "Taraf ya Nyumba ya Ngambi," *al-Islah,* October 23, 1933.

[75] "Kanuni za Kizungu, *Sharīʾa* ya Islamu na Milla ya Watu wa Africa," *al-Islah,* April 15, 1932.

[76] "Kanuni za Kizungu," Mazrui was at his sardonic best in condemning the verdict of an infamous murder trial of seventy Wakamba accused of killing a witch. For background on this case, see D. J. Penwill, *Kamba Customary Law: Notes Taken in the Machakos District of Kenya Colony* (Nairobi: East African Literature Bureau, 1972).

the decline of an Islamic knowledge economy with the decline of the Muslim elite as productive members of society, and with the decline of Arabs as knowledgeable leaders of their own religion.[77] He drew on shariʾa as a theoretical concept that could counter this decline and restore to Islam the social and cultural prestige it had enjoyed in centuries past.

Conclusion: Nationalism, Islamic Modernism, and Colonial Difference in Mombasa

In "The Scope and Limits of Islamic Cosmopolitanism," historian Muhammad Qassim Zaman takes us inside the social universe of the famous Arab traveler Ibn Battuta. Through accounts of Battuta's sojourn as a *qadi* in various Indian Ocean locales, Zaman asks us to consider not only how colonialism "invaded" the epistemic space of this cosmopolitan world, but also the hierarchical boundaries of this world and how it constituted itself through language.[78] Through close consideration of the worldview of the Sheikh al-Amin and his readers in *al-Islah,* I have tried to give an account of both of these processes.

By reimagining a binary of shariʾa/customary law in which shariʾa reinforced *kafaʾah* and custom led to a decline into *ushenzi,* Sheikh al-Amin reasserted the hegemony of Islamic cosmopolitanism in response to internal and external challenges, drawing on a mythically remembered Islamic past in East Africa in which knowledgeable and pious Arab ancestors led the community and the importance of Islamic knowledge was an unquestioned social value.[79] British colonialism shifted the epistemological basis for Indian Ocean cosmopolitanism away from Islam and the prestige of Arab genealogy to a different but equally mobile type of colonial cosmo-

---

[77] The Javanese Arab reformer Sayf al-Din al-Yemeni advanced similar arguments. See Sumit K. Mandal, "Natural Leaders of Native Muslims: Arab Ethnicity and Politics in Java Under Dutch Rule," in *Hadhrami Traders, Scholars and Statesmen in the Indian Ocean, 1750s–1960s,* ed. William G. Clarence-Smith and Ulrike Freitag (Leiden: Brill, 1997), 186–96.

[78] Muhammad Qassim Zaman, "The Scope and Limits of Islamic Cosmopolitanism and the Discursive Language of the Ulama," in *Muslim Networks: From Hajj to Hip-Hop* (Chapel Hill: University of North Carolina Press, 2005), 84.

[79] Indeed, the founder and original editor of *al-Islah,* Sheikh al-Amin Mazrui, makes frequent and repeated reference to "Wazee Wetu" (our ancestors)—a central Salafi theme—in calling upon a past ideal of Islamic community. See "Sisi na Wazee Wetu au Farka Baina Jana na Leo," *al-Islah,* April 18, 1932.

politanism; they sought to create conditions that would oblige their East African subjects to shift away from older modes of access to knowledge and power in the coastal towns.

In attempting to preserve the Islamic dimensions of Mombasa's cosmopolitanism, Sheikh al-Amin drew on a non-territorial vision of the *umma*—a global community that could be realized locally through the supremacy of shariʾa in the legal and social realm, predicated on Arab leadership. But in crafting this community through words and policies, Sheikh al-Amin and other proponents often rendered their project in the language of Arab exceptionalism. This tendency could be found elsewhere in Indian Ocean societies during this time, especially wherever Arabs had extensively intermarried with local populations.[80] While Sheikh al-Amin's reimagining of Mombasa rejected British legal norms, it relied on similar binaries between civilization and barbarism expressed through the idea that the Arab elite were the natural "leaders" of the East African Islamic community. Shariʾa was rooted in the difference between not only knowledge and ignorance, but also knowledge and barbarism.[81] Thus, if Mijikenda Muslim converts needed to learn shariʾa to fulfill their obligation in an Islamic knowledge economy, coastal Arabs needed to be knowledgeable enough to teach them. British colonialism undermined the paternalistic care at the heart of that relationship and erased the complex relationships that had helped constitute Arabs as a prestigious local community. Ironically, Sheikh al-Amin's call for a return to shariʾa and Arab leadership ignored the fact that Arabs in East Africa had been successful precisely to the degree that they had accommodated themselves to widely shared local customs and social norms. His notion of shariʾa as the rule of knowledge and justice was itself imaginary, influenced by the global refashioning of shariʾa discourse by Rida, Abduh, and their disciples.

Was there anything nationalistic about Sheikh al-Amin's vision? Rida and Abduh's ideas were closely linked to the idea of pan-Arabism and Arab nationalism, especially in Egypt. At first glance, al-Amin's writing seems to confirm Pouwels's observation that Sheikh al-Amin was acutely oriented toward the town of Mombasa. However, if we consider the

---

[80] See William G. Clarence-Smith, "Hadhramaut and the Hadhrami Diaspora in the Modern Colonial Era: An Introductory Survey," in *Hadhrami Traders, Scholars, and Statesmen,* 13. See also Ho, *Graves of Tarim,* 172.

[81] Messick, *Calligraphic State,* 166. Messick also locates shariʾa as a concept in the "control of cultural capital required for advanced instruction."

frameworks of belonging that were available to Sheikh al-Amin through Islamic modernist ideas, it is clear he attempted to map a unitary Muslim identity onto a town divided by class, race, and access to education. He imagined the *umma* much as one might imagine a nation—as a coherent, bounded public defined by its correct behavior and beliefs. His efforts at purification were also reminiscent of nationalistic thinking; he condemned practices of religion, healing, and marriage that were shared by Muslims and non-Muslims. Ironically, the impact of Sheikh al-Amin's work in Mombasa contributed to the drawing of boundaries between Muslim and non-Muslim, the maintenance of which made possible what Peter Van Der Veer refers to in an Indian context as "religious nationalism."[82] If al-Amin's thinking was not nationalist, it at least contained the threads of nationalistic thinking—threads that were products of Sheikh al-Amin's interpretation of Islamic modernist ideas through the lens of local conditions and local history.[83]

British colonialism disrupted the role of shariʾa in the coastal knowledge economy, and it did so in the midst of a vast demographic and economic transformation of Mombasa itself. In pre-colonial Mombasa, "being Arab" was associated with being knowledgeable and cultured. This formulation contained a preexisting hierarchical tension between the knowledgeable and the ignorant—the *waungwana* and the *washenzi.* Sheikh al-Amin defined what it meant to be Arab in terms of a modernist vision of shariʾa, mapping these binaries onto a more exclusive and exceptional notion of Arab identity. As the twentieth century progressed, bitter debates would erupt between Arabs and Swahili within Mombasa as this vision became more politicized.[84] Sheikh al-Amin wrote at a time when coastal Arabs in Kenya sensed their future would be dire in a Kenyan polity in which they would be a minority, not only demographically but also religiously

[82] Peter Van der Veer, *Religious Nationalism: Hindus and Muslims in India* (Berkeley: University of California Press, 1994), 57.

[83] Compare al-Amin's critique of British colonialism's legal rule in Mombasa to Partha Chatterjee's description of the activities of anti-colonial nationalism: "Colonial rule is never able to fulfill the normalizing mission of the modern state because the premise of its power is the rule of colonial difference." Partha Chatterjee, *The Nation and Its Fragments: Colonial and Postcolonial Histories* (Princeton, N.J.: Princeton University Press, 1993), 6.

[84] See, for example, the debates between Swahilis and Arabs over the origins of coastal civilization in which Arab editorial writers claim that the Arabs had "civilized" the Africans. Hyder El-Kindy, *Life and Politics in Mombasa* (Nairobi: East African Publishing House, 1972), 33.

and culturally. The precise impact of *al-Islah* on later political movements is hard to quantify, but Sheikh al-Amin did share similar anxieties about the influence and role of non-Muslims on the coast with later overtly political movements for Kenyan coastal autonomy, such as Mwambao.[85]

Works Cited

Archival Sources on Microfilm

Annual and Quarterly District Reports. Kenya National Archives Microfilm at Syracuse University.

Annual and Quarterly Reports, Coast/Seyyiddie Province. Kenya National Archives Microfilm at Syracuse University.

Daily Correspondence from Coast Province. Kenya National Archives Microfilm at Syracuse University, Series I and II.

Legislative Council Debates, Kenya National Archives Microfilm at Syracuse University.

Secretariat Circulars, Kenya National Archives Microfilm at Syracuse University.

Newspaper on Microfilm

al-Islah

Other Primary Sources

Al-Amin bin Aly. *Uwongozi.* Mombasa: East African Muslim Welfare Society, 1955.

Court of Appeal for Eastern Africa. *Law Reports Containing Decisions of the Court of Appeal for Eastern Africa.* Vol. 1 (1934). Nairobi: Government Printer, 1934.

Supreme Court. *Law Reports of Kenya Containing Cases Determined by the Supreme Court of the Colony and Protectorate of Kenya,* vols. 10–15 (1924–1933). Nairobi: Kenya Colony and Protectorate, 1953.

[85] A. I. Salim, "The Movement for 'Mwambao' or Coast Autonomy in Kenya, 1956–63," in *Hadith 2,* ed. B. A. Ogot (Nairobi: East African Publishing House, 1970), 227. See also James Brennan, "Lowering the Sultan's Flag: Sovereignty and Decolonization in Coastal Kenya," *Comparative Studies in Society and History* 50, no. 4 (2008): 831–61.

Secondary Sources

Abrahams, S. S. “The Reorganization of the Zanzibar Courts.” *Journal of Comparative Legislation and International Law,* Third Series, vol. 6, no. 4 (1924): 293–300.

Al-Farsy, Sheikh Abdullah Saleh. *The Shafi'i Ulama of East Africa, c. 1830–1970: A Hagiographic Account,* translated, edited, and annotated by Randall L. Pouwels. Madison: University of Wisconsin Program of African Studies, 1989.

Anderson, Benedict. *Imagined Communities,* new ed. London: Verso, 2006.

Appadurai, Arjun. *Modernity at Large: Cultural Dimensions of Globalization.* Minneapolis: University of Minnesota Press, 1996.

Bang, Anne. “Islamic Reform in East Africa, ca. 1870–1925: The Alawi Case.” Paper presented to the workshop "Reasserting Connections, Commonalities, and Cosmopolitanism: The Western Indian Ocean Since 1800.” Yale University, November 3–5, 2000, pp. 23–25. Available online at http://www.smi.uib.no/ab/Yale.pdf.

———. “Cosmopolitanism Colonized? Three Cases from Zanzibar 1890–1925.” In *Cosmopolitanism Contested: The Confluence of History and Anthropology in the Indian Ocean,* ed. K. Kresse and E. Simpson. London: Hurst & Co., 2007.

Berg, F. J. “Mombasa Under the Busaidi Sultanate: The City and Its Hinterlands in the Nineteenth Century.” Ph.D. diss., University of Wisconsin, 1971.

Brennan, James. “Lowering the Sultan’s Flag: Sovereignty and Decolonization in Coastal Kenya.” *Comparative Studies in Society and History* 50, no. 4 (2008): 831–61.

Caplan, Ann Patricia. *Choice and Constraint in a Swahili Community: Property, Hierarchy, and Cognatic Descent on the East African Coast.* London: Oxford University Press for the International African Institute, 1975.

Carmichael, Tim. “British ‘Practice’ Towards Islam in the East Africa Protectorate: Muslim Officials, Waqf Administration, and Secular Education in Mombasa and Environs, 1895–1920.” *Journal of Muslim Minority Affairs* 17, no. 2 (1997).

Caruso, Joseph Samuel. “Politics in Colonial Kenya, 1929–1963: A History of Kilifi District.” Ph.D. diss., Columbia University, 1993.

Chatterjee, Partha. *The Nation and Its Fragments: Colonial and Postcolonial Histories.* Princeton, N.J.: Princeton University Press, 1993.

Clarence-Smith, William G., and Ulrike Freitag, eds. *Hadhrami Traders, Scholars and Statesmen in the Indian Ocean, 1750s–1960s.* Leiden: Brill, 1997.

Cooke, Miriam, and Bruce Lawrence, eds. *Muslim Networks from Hajj to Hip Hop.* Chapel Hill: University of North Carolina Press, 2005.

Cooper, Fred. *From Slaves to Squatters: Plantation Labor and Agriculture in Zanzibar and Coastal Kenya.* Portsmouth, N.H.: Heinemann, 1997.

———. *On the African Waterfront: Urban Disorder and the Transformation of Work in Colonial Mombasa.* New Haven, Conn.: Yale University Press, 1987.

El-Kindy, Hyder. *Life and Politics in Mombasa.* Nairobi: East African Publishing House, 1972.

Ghazal, Amal. *Islamic Reform and Arab Nationalism: Expanding the Crescent from the Mediterranean to the Indian Ocean (1880s–1930s).* New York: Routledge, 2010.

Glassman, Jonathan. *Feasts and Riot: Revelry, Rebellion and Popular Consciousness on the Swahili Coast, 1856–1888.* Portsmouth, N.H.: Heinemann/James Currey, 1995.

Ho, Enseng. *Graves of Tarim: Genealogy and Mobility Across the Indian Ocean.* Berkeley: University of California Press, 2006.

Janmohamed, Karim. "Ethnicity in an Urban Setting: A Case Study of Mombasa." In *Hadith 6: History and Social Change in East Africa,* ed. B. A. Ogot, 186–206. Nairobi: East African Literature Bureau, 1976.

———. "A History of Mombasa c. 1895–1939: Some Aspects of Economic and Social Life in an East African Port Town During Colonial Rule." Ph.D. diss., Northwestern University, 1978.

Kresse, Kai. "Muslim Politics in Postcolonial Kenya: Negotiating Knowledge on the Double-Periphery." *Journal of the Royal Anthropological Institute,* special issue on "Islam, Politics and Anthropology," vol. 15, no. 1 (2009): 76–94.

Kresse, Kai, and Edward Simpson, eds. *Struggling with History: Islam and Cosmopolitanism in the Western Indian Ocean.* New York: Columbia University Press, 2008.

Lambek, Michael. "Certain Knowledge, Contestable Authority: Power and Practice on the Islamic Periphery." *American Ethnologist* 17, no. 1 (1990): 23–40.

Loimeier, Roman, and Rudiger Seesemann, eds. *Between Social Skills and Marketable Skills: The Politics of Islamic Education in 20th Century Zanzibar.* Leiden: Brill, 2009.

———. *The Global Worlds of the Swahili: Interfaces of Islam, Identity and Space in 19th and 20th-Century East Africa.* Berlin: Lit, 2006.

Martin, B. G. "Notes on Some Members of the Learned Classes of Zanzibar and East Africa in the Nineteenth Century." *African Historical Studies* 4, no. 3 (1971): 525–45.

Messick, Brinkley. *The Calligraphic State: Textual Domination and History in a Muslim Society.* Berkeley: University of California Press, 1993.

Mirza, Sara, and Margaret Strobel, eds. and trans. *Three Swahili Women: Life Histories from Mombasa, Kenya.* Bloomington: Indiana University Press, 1989.

Mraja, Mohamed S. "The Reform Ideas of Shaykh ʿAbdallāh Ṣāliḥ al-Farsī and the Transformation of Marital Practices Among Digo Muslims of Kenya." *Islamic Law and Society* 17 (2010): 245–78.

Parkin, David. *Palms, Wine and Witnesses: Public Spirit and Private Gain in an African Farming Community.* San Francisco: Chandler, 1972.

———. "The Politics of Ritual Syncretism." *Africa* 40 (1970): 217–33.

Penwill, D. J. *Kamba Customary Law: Notes Taken in the Machakos District of Kenya Colony.* Nairobi: East African Literature Bureau, 1972.

Pouwels, Randall. *Horn and Crescent: Cultural Change and Traditional Islam on the East African Coast, 800–1900.* Cambridge, Eng.: Cambridge University Press, 1987.

———. "Sh. al-Amin B. Ali Mazrui and Islamic Modernism in East Africa, 1875–1947." *International Journal of Middle East Studies* 13, no. 3 (August 1981): 329–45.

Salim, A. I. "The Movement for 'Mwambao' or Coast Autonomy in Kenya, 1956–63." In *Hadith 2,* ed. B. A. Ogot. Nairobi: East African Publishing House, 1970.

———. *The Swahili-Speaking Peoples of Kenya's Coast, 1895–1965.* Nairobi: East African Publishing House, 1973.

Soghayroun, Ibrahim E. "The Arab and Swahili Culture in Historical Perspective: Some Important Links in 'The History of the Mazrūʾīs in East Africa' by Shaykh al-Amīn b. ʿAlī al-Mazrūʿī." *Sudanic Africa* 12 (2001).

Spear, Thomas. *The Kaya Complex: A History of the Mijikenda Peoples of the Kenya Coast to 1900.* Nairobi: Kenya Literature Bureau, 1978.

Sperling, David C. "The Growth of Islam Among the Mijikenda of the Kenyan Coast, 1826–1933." Ph.D. diss., University of London, 1988.

Stren, Richard E. *Housing the Urban Poor in Africa: Policy, Politics, and Bureaucracy in Mombasa.* Berkeley: University of California, Institute of International Studies, 1977.

Strobel, Margaret. *Muslim Women in Mombasa, 1890–1975.* New Haven, Conn.: Yale University Press, 1979.

Tamim, Ghalib Yusuf. *Maisha ya Sheikh al-Amin bin Ali Mazrui (1891–1947).* Nairobi: Signal, 2005.

Van der Veer, Peter. *Religious Nationalism: Hindus and Muslims in India.* Berkeley: University of California Press, 1994.

Willis, Justin. *Mombasa, Swahili and the Making of Mijikenda.* Oxford: Clarendon, 1993.

Zein, Abdul Hamid M. *The Sacred Meadows: A Structural Analysis of Religious Symbolism in an East African Town.* Evanston, Ill.: Northwestern University Press, 1974.

"Serfs," Civics, and Social Action: Islamic Identity and Grassroots Activism during Eritrea's Tigre Emancipation Movement, 1941–1946

*Joseph L. Venosa,** SALISBURY UNIVERSITY, MARYLAND

DOI: 10.5192/215409930402165

ABSTRACT

This article examines the growth of political activism within various Tigre-speaking communities across Eritrea during the early and mid-1940s. Using previously overlooked archival as well as oral sources, it explores how some tigre "serfs" became increasingly proactive in challenging their subordinate position against local landlords, even as communities experienced a haphazard transition from Italian to temporary British colonial rule. Refusing to comply with the traditional payment of customary dues and taxes to local landlords, disenfranchised tigre across Eritrea's Western Province pressed their claims for economic and even political independence. In the process, some tigre leaders also demonstrated the complex and often problematic nature of Islamic "identity" as the emancipation movement expanded. Activists' overall success also depended upon their ability to articulate a broad, Islamic-inspired understanding of the need to rectify social and economic injustice, even though such actions challenged the existing religious institutions and authorities in the region, particularly the leadership within the dominant Khatmiyya Sufi order. Ultimately, the surge in antifeudal activism helped enrich the emerging public discourse across the colony,

*I am grateful to Professors Jonathan Miran, Tim Carmichael, and Lindsay F. Braun for providing valuable feedback on previous versions of this paper. I also thank two anonymous peer reviewers for their invaluable comments and suggestions. Any errors or mistakes herein are entirely my responsibility.

Islamic Africa, VOL. 4, NO. 2, 2013. ISSN 2154-0993. www.islamicafricajournal.org

> *which fused ideas of political independence with the need to ensure the collective security of the region's various Muslim communities, including those residing beyond the country's Tigre-speaking areas.*[1]

> The serfs or "Tigre," as they were commonly known, were as much the property of their masters, the "Shumagulle," as their camels or goats. Each "Tigre" was bound to an individual "Shumagulle"; he and his songs passed in inheritance to the descendents of his Shumagulle; and at the will of his Shumagulle he could be sold, given away, punished by flogging, or put to death.[2]

For many communities across Eritrea's Western Province, the transition from five decades of Italian colonial rule to British control in April 1941 presented an opportunity to rework the traditional social and economic constraints under which most residents had lived for nearly three centuries. British rule in Eritrea came as a result of Allied military operations during World War II, as Italian forces across the colony were overrun by British-led Allied regiments in early 1941, less than a year after Italy's invasion of eastern Sudan. Although Eritreans as a whole found themselves living within the confines of a new colonial authority with the coming of Allied forces in April 1941, those on the lower rungs of Tigre-speaking society—known specifically and pejoratively as *tigre* at the time—adapted particularly well to new realities and opportunities under the British Military Administration (BMA) between 1941 and 1952. While tigre discontent toward regional landlords (known as *shumagulle,* and also Tigre-speakers) had surfaced during the earlier periods of Turko-Egyptian and Italian rule, the period of BMA authority marked the beginning of a

---

[1] Portions of this paper appear in the following publications: Joseph L. Venosa, "Paths Toward the Nation: Islamic Identity, the Eritrean Muslim League, and Nationalist Mobilization, 1941–61" (Ph.D. diss., Ohio University, 2011); "Adapting to the New Path: Khatmiyya Sufi Authority, the al-Mirghani Family, and Eritrean Nationalism During British Occupation, 1941–1949," *Journal of Eastern African Studies* 7, no. 3 (2013): 413–31.

[2] *Papers of Sir Kennedy Trevaskis,* Box 1 (b), "The Tigre-Speaking Peoples," 126, MSS Brit Emp S. 367, Bodleian Library of Commonwealth & African Studies at Rhodes House, Oxford University. Henceforth cited as *Trevaskis Papers.* While the term "tigre" referred to someone of servant status, it eventually developed into a wider marker for the ethnocultural identity for all those, vassal and shumagulle alike, who came from Tigre-speaking areas. In the context of this article, "tigre" in lowercase spelling refers to those of "serf" or vassal status.

greater crystallization in tigre class identity, and a major shift in how activists challenged local *religious* institutions and authorities as a means of achieving reform.[3]

This article argues that the growing emancipation movement across tigre communities during the early and mid-1940s represented a major watershed in Eritrea's eventual push toward decolonization, as activists simultaneously challenged both the traditional landlord-serf dynamic within Eritrea as well as the system's exploitation by colonial authorities. Ultimately, many of the leaders in the emancipation movement also articulated new understandings of tigre identity that stressed the righteousness of their cause as devout Muslims and the necessity of breaking away from the "feudalism" of the shumagulle, whom many tigre viewed as being less than genuine in their Islamic practices. In addition, this article offers an overview of how varying interpretations of tigre Islamic identity also adapted to broader institutional and social changes as Eritrea transitioned from Italian to British colonial rule.

Tigre-Speaking Eritrea and the Historical Tigre-Shumagulle Divide

While Tigre was the dominant language across what is now western and northern Eritrea, other groups, including Bedawi (Beja)-speaking peoples and smaller ethno-cultural groups—particularly the Kunama and Nara—lived in close proximity across the region. Tigre- and Beja-speaking groups nevertheless dominated the area, forming an "approximate triangle, at its widest extending to areas between Zula (south of Massawa), Tokar (south of Sawākin), and the areas of the modern western border between Eritrea and Sudan."[4] Within Eritrea proper, Tigre-speaking communities dominated the lowland areas from coastal regions in southern Semhar, around coastal cities such as Massawa and Hirgigo, and toward the interior regions over most of the modern-day regions of Gash-Barka and Anseba in the west. Historically, the various Tigre-speaking peoples were divided

[3] In general, transliterated Arabic terms have followed a simplified version of the most recent guidelines set forth by the *International Journal of Middle East Studies.* Likewise, individual names, places, and technical terms originating among Eritrea's Tigre-speaking communities have been rendered in the standardized form most familiar to English speakers. Unless otherwise noted, all translations are my own.

[4] Jonathan Miran, "Constructing and Deconstructing the Tigre Frontier Space in the Long Nineteenth Century," in *History and Language of the Tigre-Speaking Peoples,* ed. Gianfrancesco Lusini (Naples: Università degli Studi di Napoli "L'Orientale," 2010), 37.

"into a number of tribes and tribal confederations" and included groups such as the Beni-Amer of the western lowlands; the Marya, Bet Juk, and a large part of the Mensa' group all residing in the area around Keren; and groups such as the Habab, ʿAd Takles, ʿAd Temaryam, and the ʿAd Muʾallim of the northern highlands.[5]

The subservient relationship between tigre and their shumagulle "masters" stood at the heart of economic, social, and to an extent religious life across Tigre-speaking society.[6] Much of the scholarship traces the origins of this master-serf relationship to the arrival of several of the Bet Asghede clans during the sixteenth century. The Bet Asghede, who spoke Tigrinya and practiced Orthodox Tewahado Christianity, migrated into the region from the Eritrean highlands (*kebessa*) as part of the broader "Ethiopian" conquest that subdued most of the regional clans and reorganized political and social authority across the territory. Ultimately, this migration resulted in most Tigre-speaking groups being subjected to a "small Christian aristocracy" that increasingly refined social divisions throughout the next three centuries by dominating access to land, foodstuffs, and livestock.[7]

Thus, while most of the Bet Asghede clans eventually converted to Islam and adopted the Tigre language by the late eighteenth century, their origins and agro-pastoralist lifestyle solidified their place as a separate and privileged minority within Tigre-speaking society. Over time this developed into a quasi-aristocratic arrangement in which elite families, known as *shumagulle,* came to dominate the mainly pastoralist Tigre-speaking groups. Control of the land and its resources came to embody the primary means of both wealth and status for the shumagulle, as the ruling families increasingly kept to a settled life within the encampments (*digge*) under the direct authority of their respective clan chief. Nevertheless, the majority of tigre residents played an essential role during the first two centuries as laborers and key suppliers of livestock and raw goods in exchange for shumagulle protection and access to grazing lands.

Although the relationship between a tigre and a shumagulle depended

---

[5] Ibid.

[6] See Abba Isaak Ghebre Iyesus, *Arguments for Shedding Some Light on the Tîgré Phenomenon,* trans. Amanuel Sahle (Asmara: MBY Press, 1996), 30–37; Alberto Pollera, *Le Popolazioni Indigene dell'Eritrea* (Bologna: L. Capelli, 1935), 196–97, 226–27; Carlo Conti Rossini, *Principli di Diritto Consuetudinario dell'Eritrea* (Rome: Tipografia Dell'Unione Editrice, 1916), 541–721.

[7] *Trevaskis Papers,* Box 1 (b), "The Tigre-Speaking Peoples," 13.

upon the latter's position as the proprietor of the land and its resources, relations between the two groups also varied according to clan, community size, and the nature of the local subsistence economy. Nevertheless, a basic continuity in the Tigre-speaking region solidified throughout the eighteenth and nineteenth centuries. The differences in both livelihood and community organization helped establish the shumagulle and tigre as two distinct social groups that filled very different roles within Tigre-speaking society. Although the major clans (*qebelaat*) identified both the shumagulle and tigre as belonging to the group, many tigre viewed themselves as belonging to a series of smaller sub-clans, or "races," that lived in proximity to one another and under the larger clan markers such as the Bet Asghede, ʿAd Takles, Bet Jut, and others.[8]

Local variables and clan markers notwithstanding, certain aspects of the relationship between tigre and shumagulle were universal. The tigre who worked the land paid customary dues to the shumagulle landholder in the form of either livestock or locally harvested foodstuffs, but could not engage in debate or argue with his shumagulle, negotiate the terms of the traditional land "contract," or terminate the relationship. Shumagulle could also expect their tigre vassals to provide unpaid supplemental labor when needed. Usually this included agricultural work, the milking of animals, and fetching firewood and other supplies. The shumagulle also reserved the right to use tigre livestock for cultivation and other animals, such as camels and mules, for their own transportation needs.[9] Keren's Senior Civil Affairs Officer (SCAO) Kennedy Trevaskis, who arguably became the most knowledgeable BMA official involved with tigre-shumagulle relations, also took note of the peculiarities of the relationship, remarking during his tenure in the region that "even where the relationship between tigre and shumagulle was reasonably cordial, the two classes remained castes immutably divided from each other."[10]

[8] At the height of tigre discontent, representatives claimed that more than one hundred subgroups existed across the territory. *Trevaskis Papers,* Box 2 (a), *Four Power Commission of Investigation for the Former Italian Colonies,* Report on Eritrea, "Letter of Tigré Representatives," Appendix 18, 3. The Four Power Commission, a group composed of representatives from Britain, France, the United States, and the Soviet Union, first convened talks in London in September 1945 to discuss the future of Italy's former colonial territories, including Eritrea. It was not until November 1947 that representatives arrived in Eritrea on a fact-finding mission to ascertain local political attitudes.

[9] Alemseged Tesfai, *Aynfelale: 1941–1950* (Asmara: Hidri, 2002), 69–74.

[10] *Trevaskis Papers,* Box 1 (b), "The Tigre-Speaking Peoples," 128.

Sufi Influence and Regional Islamic Institutions

The region comprising the heart of Tigre-speaking Eritrea experienced several waves of Islamic diffusion starting in the first half of the eighth century, with the majority of residents of the western lowlands and the affiliated coastal region adopting Islam during the thirteenth century. This conversion from Tewahado Orthodox Christianity to Sunni Islam occurred mainly due to the growth of the regional sea-based trade routes and the travels of pious Muslims from across the Arabian Peninsula.[11] Despite a variety of Islamic influences over time, the most important and dynamic effect on Muslim practices and institutional organization prior to colonialism came in the nineteenth century from several revivalist movements around the Red Sea. These movements spurred the travels of an assortment of itinerant preachers and members of Sufi orders.[12] Ultimately these developments solidified Islam among the majority of the lowland population to a point where, by the middle of the nineteenth century, virtually all Tigre-speaking groups had adopted Islam.[13] Intensified proselytization among the Sufi groups and holy families within the various segments of tigre society effectively created an "Islamic Space" throughout the region.[14]

Two Islamic entities in particular, the ʿAd Shaykh holy family and the Khatmiyya order, ultimately provided much of the momentum of this later revivalism by dominating Islamic religious practices and gaining new converts among the tigre population. Originally of Meccan origin, the members of the ʿAd Shaykh family established themselves in Eritrea during the early nineteenth century and successfully won over large segments of tigre. Together with their *naʾib* allies along the Eritrean coast, they brought locals into their ranks as members of the Qadiriyya Sufi brotherhood.[15] With

[11] Jonathan Miran, *Red Sea Citizens: Cosmopolitan Society and Cultural Change in Massawa* (Bloomington: Indiana University Press, 2009), 170.

[12] See John O. Voll, "A History of the Khatmiyyah Tariqah in the Sudan" (Ph.D. diss., Harvard University, 1969).

[13] Miran, *Red Sea Citizens,* 30.

[14] Miran, "Constructing and Deconstructing the Tigre Frontier Space in the Long Nineteenth Century," 43. Miran also argues that in spite of the regional consolidation of the various Sufi *taruq* (a plural of the term *tariqa* [path or way], *taruq* refers to a particular school of sufi Islamic thought; several Sufi Islamic orders are also often referred to as *taruq*), the political dynamics within much of Tigre society remained "multifaceted and protean." Ibid., 50. See also Ghebre Iyesus, *Arguments for Shedding Some Light on the Tigré Phenomenon.*

[15] *Naʾib,* or "deputy," refers to the historical group of "Beja-descended Balaws" that developed widespread influence over local Muslim authorities and extended their power in the area between the Eritrean Red Sea coast and the highland plateau until the mid-nineteenth

the coming of the ʿAd Shaykh holy family during the early nineteenth century, most of the shumagulle converted to Islam despite the fact that "many of their serfs and more especially the subject Almada [*sic*] peoples were Moslems either by long tradition or later conversion."[16] This late "turn to Islam" by the dominant class provided activists with additional validation that their status as a true Muslim people justified their moral struggle for emancipation, fostering the argument that "we could call it an evolution in the opposite sense, as not we, the dependents, have adopted religion, language and customs of the dominating people, but they, the dominating class have adopted our religion, language and customs."[17] This perspective on the "inauthentic" religious and moral standing of the shumagulle helps explain why many tigre representatives eventually rejected the legitimacy of the elites as true Muslims. Indeed, much of the later justification for tigre emancipation that emerged during the 1940s included references to the fact that, in the past, the majority of the shumagulle had been Christian until the Islamic revivals of the early nineteenth century.[18]

While the ʿAd Shaykhs' success continued along much of the coastal lowlands, western and northern Eritrea experienced an equally significant diffusion of Islamic revivalism from the growing influence of the Khatmiyya order under the leadership of the al-Mirghani family. Founded by Muhammad ʿUthman al-Mirghani (1793–1852), the Khatmiyya's success in developing their membership and allegiance with both urban and

century. See Jonathan Miran, "Power Without Pashas: The Anatomy of Naʾib Autonomy in Ottoman Eritrea (17th–19th C.)," *Eritrean Studies Review* 5, no. 1 (2007): 33–88.

[16] *Trevaskis Papers,* Box 1 (b), "The Tigre-Speaking Peoples," 19.

[17] "To H.E. Brigadier C. D'arcy Mc. Carthy O.B.E. Chief Administrator- Eritrea- Asmara," 9, BMA/DIS 260/kel 10957/89, Research and Documentation Center (RDC), Asmara, Eritrea. Henceforth cited as RDC. A report composed by the Four Power Commission in 1947 also took note of this distinction. The report noted that it was "strange how these Christian Abyssinian populations, instead of attracting the inhabitants of the territories occupied by them, were themselves attracted by the subjected populations whose language and religion they absorbed." *Trevaskis Papers,* Box 2 (a), *Four Power Commission of Investigation for the Former Italian Colonies,* Report on Eritrea, "The Question of the Tigré," Appendix 17, 2.

[18] *Trevaskis Papers,* Box 2 (a), *Four Power Commission of Investigation for the Former Italian Colonies,* Report on Eritrea, "Letter of Tigré Representatives," Appendix 18, 3–4. Tigre representatives' claims were, however, complicated by the fact that the rise of the Khatmiyya-sponsored "revival" during the nineteenth century among the ʿAd Shaykh and ʿAd Muʾallim had essentially reconverted even these already-Islamicized tigre. See Miran, "Constructing and Deconstructing the Tigre Frontier Space in the Long Nineteenth Century," 44.

especially rural communities has been attributed to the brotherhood's ability to incorporate many of the preexisting religious formations, including notable families and holy lineages, into a "supra-community network" that had far-reaching social consequences.[19] Across the region, Khatmiyya authorities became essential to the functions of the several hundred Sufi lodges (*zawaya*) and Qur'anic schools (*khalwaat*) that existed across the region. These localized Islamic institutions helped ensure that the order maintained a strong presence in conducting religious duties, providing Arabic language instruction, and training younger generations for positions within the order. The Khatmiyya's rise across the region meant that traditional "customary laws" involving the payment of debts, the settlement of feuds, inheritances, and other customs also fell under the oversight of Khatmiyya leaders. As a result, Sufi authorities increasingly placed *qadis* and affiliated *khalifas* in key positions to arbitrate disputes, effectively reorienting customary law under direct oversight of Islamic clergy. This resulted in Khatmiyya-backed religious courts becoming an integral part of civil authority, making their role in upholding the traditional social divisions all the more important for securing their own place as the region's major Islamic authority.

Yet Khatmiyya influence also extended beyond the realm of religious authority and institutional governance, into the social and economic fabric of everyday life for Muslim communities. In particular, many *khalifas* within the order served in important roles as merchants and wholesalers in major cities such as Keren, Tessenei, and Agordat, where they played an integral role in facilitating trade between eastern Sudan and coastal trading zones along the Red Sea.[20] Because of the order's long-standing success across the region in co-opting community leaders and elite family structures throughout the late nineteenth century, much of what became the Western Province effectively came under Khatmiyya economic control as Sufi leaders utilized their religious influence to facilitate economic relations between Eritrean communities and those members across the border in nearby Kassala, the eastern Sudanese city and center of the order's activities.[21]

This resulted in the order having a high degree of public visibility and institutional authority among community members, including both

[19] Miran, *Red Sea Citizens,* 178.

[20] Aberra Osman Aberra, interview with author, Columbus, Ohio, July 23, 2010.

[21] See *Trevaskis Papers,* Box 1 (b), "The Tigre-Speaking Peoples," 12–36, 120–40.

urban-based residents and those engaged in agro-pastoralism in the more rural areas. This also meant that, on a grassroots level, Khatmiyya leaders increasingly became key partners in reinforcing social divisions and in helping regulate relations between tigre and shumagulle. Some observers noted that the Khatmiyya's importance in maintaining these divisions only reinforced the perception among most rank and file tigre that the order's primary purpose involved using control of everyday Islamic institutions to guarantee obedience and minimize dissent. Commenting on the order's dominance across the region during the early 1940s, Eritrea's highest-ranking Islamic official, Grand Mufti Ibrahim al-Mukhtar, noted that in addition to wielding such a large economic and political role, the al-Mirghani family and its closest supporters often removed those Islamic religious officials "who didn't toe their line" on doctrinal issues and replaced them with loyalists within the order, even if they lacked any legitimate qualifications or training in the Islamic sciences.[22]

Born in 1909 near Mount Kended in Akkele Guzay Province, Ibrahim al-Mukhtar came from a family with a legacy of involvement in Islamic religious affairs across the region. Many of his family members within the Saho-speaking Harak Faqih subclan served as prominent Islamic scholars and jurists in the area. Utlimately, Ibrahim al-Mukhtar's travels across the region during the early 1940s revealed the fragmented nature of the colony's Islamic communities and demonstrated the extent to which Islamic practices across the Western Province in particular were under Khatmiyya control. Nevertheless, the quality and rigor of Islamic institutions and their respective personnel were less of a concern for most tigre activists, who argued that such deficiencies only further demonstrated how high-ranking religious officials had failed in their duty to alter the plight of the landless majority at the hands of the shumagulle. Indeed, ongoing political conflict between the tigre and the shumagulle reflected how the Islamic revivals and establishment of Italian colonial rule during the late nineteenth century actually reinforced their respective exclusion.

Historically, the divide between tigre and shumagulle involved a complex system of political authority within the communities. While many tigre groups were traditionally served by a council of elders, or *mahaber,* that tied them together, the shumagulle-led positions of chief (*shum*) and subchief (*hisset*) also developed into markers of respect despite the fact that the real legislative and judicial authority "lay with the 'mahaber' and

[22] Ismael al-Mukhtar, electronic correspondence with author, Athens, Ohio, October 14, 2009.

not with the Shum personally, although he would act as its spokesmen and leader."[23] These political roles existed alongside prevailing authorities within the Khatmiyya, where *khalifas* often served simultaneously as religious officials while working in key positions as chiefs, sub-chiefs, and tax collectors.[24] By exercising both religious influence and political authority within these positions, shumagulle also benefited economically from such arrangements, as landlords used their position within the clans to utilize other community resources for their benefit. One of the most common intersections of Khatmiyya-shumagulle power developed out of the structure of the regional *waqf* system.[25]

Across Eritrea's Western Province, authority over the designation and maintenance of these Islamic religious endowments often developed into a system of patronage that linked the religious, political, and social authority of shumagulle leaders. Many tigre activists openly complained that the Khatmiyya's shumagulle-affiliated *khalifas* had abused the institution of the *waqf* by either transferring or selling community properties to their own relatives at the expense of the wider public. Across the Western Province, rural tigre—those whose existence was fundamentally tied to having access to land and the use of community property—became some of the most vocal activists to accuse shumagulle leaders of their "perversions" of Islamic practices. Tigre criticisms were later addressed directly by Ibrahim al-Mukhtar. By mid-1943, as settlements across the Western Province faced increased instability due to activists, the mufti (with official BMA support) took control of the colony's various *waqf* committees in an effort to both reform the institutions from Khatmiyya patronage and to expunge those religious officials who displayed supposed "lax Islamic practices."[26] With newfound authority to directly appoint members to the *waqf* committees across major cities and towns, the mufti soon issued

---

[23] *Trevaskis Papers,* Box 1 (b), "The Tigre-Speaking Peoples," 137. The term "Kantiba" also designated the status of the ruling chief recognized within most Tigre-speaking clans. See Anthony D'Avray, *The Nakfa Documents: The Despatches, Memoranda, Reports, and Correspondence Describing and Explaining the Stories of the Feudal Societies of the Red Sea Littoral from the Christian-Muslim Wars of the Sixteenth Century to the Establishment 1885–1901 of the Italian Colony of Eritrea* (Wiesbaden: Harrassowitz Verlag, 2000), 2.

[24] Aberra Osman Aberra, interview.

[25] A *waqf* (plural *awqaf*) is generally defined within Islamic law as a religious endowment. It usually corresponds to a donation made in the form of a specific building, house, or property to be used for religious and/or charitable purposes.

[26] Ismael al-Mukhtar, interview.

edicts "whereby each *sharia qadi* of the principal towns was vested with the power of establishing an *awqaf* committee and appointing its members in his administrative jurisdiction."[27] Although the mufti and his closet supporters often had to "walk a fine line" in implementing the institutional reforms without directly challenging leading members of the al-Mirghani family, the reforms nevertheless dovetailed with tigre activism at a key point in the movement. A growing number of tigre—especially those who had left the rural territories and emerged as part of the small urban professional class—became increasingly supportive of efforts to "standardize" Islamic practices within the mosques, *awqaf,* and *khalwaat,* as well as to guard against unwarranted shumagulle influence within religious institutions. Although the mufti and his inner circle did not explicitly come out in support of tigre emancipation during the early 1940s, the nature of the reforms and his own reputation as both an Islamic scholar and an official far-removed from tigre-shumagulle tensions gave him a degree of credibility that only increased throughout the decade.[28]

Tigre Activism and the BMA Response

While limited uprisings against landowners had occurred throughout Italian colonial rule and surfaced with particular intensity during the 1920s and 1930s, by mid-1941 the situation of most tigre had worsened beyond even the dire conditions that communities experienced under Fascist rule. This deterioration was due in part to the increased economic burden placed on rural Eritrea after Italy's invasion of Ethiopia in 1935, and especially to Italy's decision to invade Sudan in June 1940. With the combined stresses of a wartime economy, the need for manpower and resources, and the power vacuum brought on by the end of formal Italian rule, many tigre again began refusing to pay customary dues to their respective shumagulle.[29]

Thus, the BMA's arrival in Eritrea occurred at one of the most problematic periods in the colony's history, as emerging social and economic challenges confronted British administrators even before they had secured

---

[27] Ibrahim al-Mukhtar, "The Position of the Mufti on Tribal and Religious Differences," Ismael al-Mukhtar, http://www.mukhtar.ca/contentN.php?type=viewarticle&id=139&category=mawakef_mukhtar (accessed June 10, 2010).

[28] Ibid.

[29] See Tesfai, *Aynfelale,* 69–74.

the entire territory from Italian control. Faced with their own financial and personnel shortages, British administrators kept much of the previous Italian colonial civil service intact while trying to placate the nearly 70,000 Italian settlers residing in the territory.[30] Consequently, the BMA proved both unable and unwilling to seriously entertain any discussion of political and economic reform among Eritrea's indigenous population, particularly among the Tigre-speaking communities of the Western Province. Nevertheless, colonial officers were forced to address tigre concerns at the outset of the BMA's establishment in the spring of 1941. Initially, in May, tigre living under the control of Bet Asghede in the Western Province's Keren Division petitioned BMA authorities for their support in the enforcement of "their rights" against shumagulle abuse. Specifically, representatives requested immediate British protection against both the physical and financial abuse of the landowners, whom they viewed as attempting to extract unreasonable amounts of tribute and customary dues from the tigre at a time of increased hardship.[31] Shumagulle representatives also approached the British, claiming that the refusals to pay tribute had prevented them from executing their traditional duties as clan chiefs. Many shumagulle also claimed that their very livelihood depended on receiving the customary tribute.[32] At first, BMA officials attempted to maneuver carefully between both groups so as to not risk any major social disruption. In December 1941, however, the situation worsened when tigre representatives announced they would refuse to give the traditional payment (*magasa*) of one-fourth of the coming harvest to the shumagulle.[33] In February 1942, British personnel met with shumagulle and tigre representatives and informed the interested parties that because officials believed the land "was vested in the Government," the already understaffed administration would not legally recognize or enforce the collection of traditional dues by the shumagulle. In response, shumagulle from the Bet Asghede threatened to evict all tigre from their land if they refused to make their payments.[34]

Refusal to pay customary dues presented British administrators with a serious problem. While administrators recognized their own reliance

[30] See *The First to Be Freed: The Record of British Military Administration in Eritrea and Somalia, 1941–43* (London: His Majesty's Stationery Office, 1944), 6–48.

[31] Trevaskis, "Dispute Between the Shumagulle and Tigre of the Ad Takles," 1, BMA/DIS 260/kel 10957/62, RDC, Asmara.

[32] Major Lea, "Major Lea to the Military Administrator, O.E.T.A, Eritrea," 4, BMA/DIS 260/kel 10957/1, RDC, Asmara.

[33] Ibid., 1.

[34] Trevaskis, "Dispute Between the Shumagulle and Tigre of the Ad Takles," 1.

on the shumagulle as instruments of revenue collection and authority, the prospect of mass civil disobedience by the tigre encouraged BMA authorities to seek a compromise. Indeed, the BMA's relatively rich documentation of tigre activity and the political and economic implications of its policies demonstrates that the colonial administration, while short-lived, nevertheless provided the best documentary evidence of such transformations. Because of the relative lack of written and oral testimony about the tigre movement from most of the direct participants—particularly those involved during the early protests prior to 1946—BMA testimonies represent one of the most valuable assortments of texts that document both the activists' demands and the movement's broader implications across Tigre-speaking society. In light of the fact that scholars have yet to investigate the emancipation movement in any significant detail, BMA sources provide an important perspective on how tigre activists themselves viewed the importance of Islam and religious identity to their cause.

Rejecting suggestions that the traditional land dues be declared illegal and that all "tribal land" instead be considered government land, British officials in general supported a more moderate policy of allowing the customary payment of one-fourth of their harvest, with additional continued payments only if they were "rendered voluntarily by a tigre to his Shamagulle." Trevaskis argued that the administrators should "sanction no change of individual ownership" of traditional shumagulle lands, and added that no tigre could be evicted from a residence unless this was approved by the presiding civil affairs officer.[35] In trying to contain tigre discontent by promising greater oversight for the payment of customary dues, Trevaskis's plan won the support of Eritrea's then Chief Administrator, Brigadier Stephen Longrigg. Having considered the range of possible actions on the tigre land issue, Longrigg summarized the need for a cautious policy:

> The abolition by a "stroke of the pen" of all feudal dues, much as we may recommend it on general grounds, cannot be upheld. Such a change, which would have far reaching repercussions, must go hand in hand with a general re-organization of tribal society—its tributary system, political representation, etc. The present time is hardly suitable for such far-reaching schemes.[36]

---

[35] Ibid.

[36] Stephen Longrigg, "Dispute Between Shumagulle and Tigre," 7, BMA/DIS 260/kel 109577, RDC, Asmara.

Although by June 1943 the BMA had fully articulated a policy that recognized shumagulle authority while promising to increase oversight to guarantee the tigres' "protection and security of tenure" against possible abuse, the movement to sever the traditional subservience proved inadequate. Rather than petitioning to simply redress the terms of the traditional payments, activists sought to guarantee their independence from conditions that many tigre viewed as nothing short of slavery.[37]

Despite the BMA's apparent initial success in holding a public assembly for shumagulle and tigre representatives in the city of Keren in late June, the possibility that some of the most influential tigre activists would not be willing to compromise stoked administrative fears. In particular, they worried about the actions of Keren resident Mohamed Hamid Tahgé, who emerged as the leader of a small group of tigre activists within the ᶜAd Takles clan. While British reports alleged that Tahgé himself did not cultivate land due to his job as a trader, he gained a loyal following among the ᶜAd Takles with his bold public assertions that he would "rather die than allow a single *rubaiya* of *dura* [wheat] to be paid over to the Bet Asghede (Shamagulle)."[38] Tahgé's early activism as a spokesman for ᶜAd Takles set a precedent within the larger tigre movement; coming from the ranks of the local tigre communities, most of the representatives who gained prominence as leaders often did not own land themselves, but instead were members of the colonial-educated intelligentsia in nearby cities.[39]

By fall, as shumagulle and tigre from the ᶜAd Takles continued to feud, the BMA called a meeting between Tahgé's faction and shumagulle representatives in order to come to an agreement about the traditional payment of one-fourth of the crops. Tahgé and his colleagues not only refused to pay any portion of the allotted sum, but they also told BMA officials that they had publicly encouraged all of their fellow tigre to do the same. The British report of the meeting alleges that Tahgé stated that he preferred to be exiled to the city of Assab as punishment for his actions than to "pay one grain of *dura* to the Shumagallé."[40] For the next three years, Tahgé and his group embodied both the resilience of tigre resolve as well as the ba-

---

[37] "Tigre-Shumagalle Dispute," 1, BMA/DIS 260/kel 10957/68, RDC, Asmara.

[38] "Land Disputes (Shumagulle v. Tigre: Ad Takles)," 1, BMA/DIS 260/kel 10957/15, RDC, Asmara. He is also listed in BMA records as Hamed Humid Tahge and Hamid Humed Tei.

[39] In later years, Tahgé continued his political efforts and became a leading representative of the Eritrean Muslim League's Keren branch.

[40] "Report on Ad Tacles & Shumagulle-Tigre Dispute," 1, K/66/b/6, RDC, Asmara.

sic dilemma for British officials of dealing with growing unrest. Although Tahgé and his colleagues were exiled to Assab for over a year until mid-1945, officials had little success establishing a truce between the remaining tigre and shumagulle representatives.[41]

In a February 1945 appeal to officials stationed in the Keren Division, Tahgé and his tigre colleagues Mohammed Ali Suleiman and Idris Faʾid Hummed continued to reject the BMA's ruling requiring tigre to pay one-fourth of their harvest. They argued that "as this has never been practiced beforehand we are not prepared to do it now we ask Y.E. [your Excellency] for justice and consideration in this case."[42] Perhaps not surprisingly, some elements within the BMA recognized that the fundamental conflict between tigre and landholders could not be resolved with reconciliatory measures or by attempting to institute modest payment proposals. Reflecting on the ongoing troubles with tigre exiles in Assab, the presiding district officer provided a lucid summation of the BMA's general attitude:

> These men, with whom I have had a long and at times most irritating acquaintance, are leaders of the Ad Takles [*sic*] Tigre. They are local "Wat Tylers" and rebels against a political and social system which can in no way recommend itself to an enlightened European. We are however obliged for reasons of administrative expediency to preserve this system and to prevent any "Peasants' Revolt."[43]

Ironically, in spite of the BMA's issuing of the exile order, the "ʿAd Takles Group" refused to discontinue its activities. Officials noted in May 1945 that between February and May Tahgé himself took up residence in Asmara, where he was "frequenting the offices" of a local lawyer of tigre origins for advice on the issue.[44] For his part, Idris Faʾed Hummed continued his travels among the ʿAd Takles community, where he allegedly took

---

[41] "Petition–Hamid Humed Taʾe and others," 1, BMA/DIS 260/kel 10957/85, RDC, Asmara. The agreement, dated June 16, 1944, also included the signatures of colleagues Abdalla Ibrahim, Ali Tulug, Hamad Humed, and Idris Omer.

[42] "Appeal," 1, BMA/DIS 260/kel 10957/86, RDC, Asmara. According to BMA reports, Mohammed Ali Suleiman and Idris Faʾid Hummed served in the Italian colonial civil service during the previous decade and by the early 1940s had developed commercial links in Keren while maintaining close ties to their kin within the predominantly rural ʿAd Takles communities.

[43] "Ad Takles Exiles in Assab," 1, BMA/DIS 260/kel 10957/105, RDC, Asmara.

[44] By all accounts, the lawyer in question was tigre activist Ibrahim Sultan.

an even more active role than before by "constantly preaching to the Tigre on their alleged oppression and the injustice of having to pay rent on the land."[45] This included discussions with regional *qadis* and students within the various *khalwaat,* whom Hummed implored to follow their "duties" as Muslims to speak out against their treatment by joining the emancipation cause.[46]

Beyond the inability of administrators to come to terms with the complexities of levying appropriate customary dues, many British officials believed that a substantial portion of the shumagulle lived in conditions of abject poverty and could not survive without the payment of tribute. A December 1941 report surmised that "the trouble in the Asgade tribes is that the Sciumagalle [*sic*] are mostly so miserably poor in animals that their customary dues are their livelihood."[47] Nearly four years later, Keren's presiding SCAO echoed this idea and claimed that the shumagulle's apparent domination was largely inflated; in fact, he asserted, many of the landowners worked the land "side by side with the Tigre," and many were so poor that they were forced to sell some of their surplus land.[48] Political scientist John Markakis also supports this claim, stating that the shumagulle's vulnerable position developed partially as a result of the nature of the local agricultural economy. For several years, the growth of the tigre population resulted in a large increase in livestock and overall agricultural capabilities that helped transform many of the supposedly subservient tigre into a group "often wealthier than the nobles."[49] In a report issued in December 1945, one BMA administrator claimed that although he felt Mohamed Ali Suleiman and Idris Faʾid could return from exile in Assab to the Western Province during the raining season (spring) of 1946, he cautioned against allowing Tahgé to return because it could jeopardize BMA efforts to quell the unrest. The memo also referenced the apparent British sympathy for the shumagulle, whom they viewed as being "very poor" and unable to subsist without the mandated payments.[50]

Nevertheless, "emancipatory" activism progressed throughout the

[45] "Tigre/Shumagalle Dispute-Ad Tekles," 1, BMA/DIS 260/kel 10957/94, RDC, Asmara.

[46] Ibid.

[47] "Memo from Major Lea to Military Administrator, O.E.T.A, Eritrea," 4, BMA/DIS 260/kel 10957/1, RDC, Asmara.

[48] "Ad Takles Exiles," 1, BMA/DIS 260/kel 10957/113, RDC, Asmara.

[49] John Markakis, *National and Class Conflict in the Horn of Africa* (Cambridge, Eng.: Cambridge University Press, 1987), 59.

[50] "Ad Takles Exiles," 1.

region with increased vigor. One of the more dramatic episodes occurred in early 1943, when a tigre from the Rugbat clan, Humid Shentub, purportedly killed a shumagulle during a confrontation after the landowners told Shentub to vacate his plot in the village of Tselim Dengel for refusing to pay tribute.[51] If some representatives thought that openly refusing payment could end tigre subservience and a few were moved to violence, some also believed that the best way to solve the crisis was social reorganization. In January 1944, Major R. Signals reported from Keren that authorities had imprisoned five tigre from the ʿAd Takles on the grounds that they had illegally collected goats, *dura,* and money from serf families while "inciting people to disobey the Administration by breaking away from their tribes and forming a tribe of their own under the name of Asghede."[52] Commenting on the apparent widespread support for their actions, the report noted that all of the residents of the local tigre clans "have taken an oath that they will not give evidence in court against the five above-named accused."[53] Concerned that the tigre from the ʿAd Takles and other clans could realistically break away from the "Shumagelle-ruled tribes" and form their own "autonomous section," the BMA looked to local Islamic authorities to try and end the turmoil.

Islamic Authorities and Unrest in the Tigre Frontier

Echoing their earlier role as an intermediate authority between the general population and Italian administrators during the nineteenth and early twentieth centuries, the Khatmiyya hierarchy initially served as an important resource for BMA officials in establishing both control and allegiance across the region throughout 1941. This influence reflected the continued significance of Sufi authorities, which centered on the lodges and schools as "crystallizing spaces and circuits of religious and social confluence among Muslims chiefly in the tigre region."[54] Ever mindful of the religious

---

[51] Ibrahim Sultan allegedly came to Shentu's aid while the latter was imprisoned and sentenced to pay compensation for his act. Despite Shentu's imprisonment, Sultan launched a public campaign in his defense across the Western Province. See Tesfai, *Aynfelale,* 73–74.

[52] Major R. Signals, "Mohammed Nur Mohammed Abdulla, Mohammed Suleiman Idris Nur, Ismael Sicap, Mohammed Adam Abdulla, Hamid Said Osman," 1, BMA/DIS 260/kel 10957/32, RDC, Asmara.

[53] Ibid.

[54] Miran, "Constructing and Deconstructing the Tigre Frontier Space in the Long Nineteenth Century," 44.

dynamics across the northern highlands, Trevaskis noted their influence early on during his tenure in Keren:

> Today the whole of this bloc of Moslem, and Tigre speaking, communities are culturally united not only by the fact that they are almost all Moslem, but also by the fact that (together with many communities in the Sudan) they adhere to the Tariga al-Khatmia [*sic*], the religious "path" or sect founded by Said Mohammad Osman El Mirghani [*sic*], a descent of the Prophet, who died in the Northern Sudan in 1853.[55]

Nevertheless, as calls for tigre emancipation grew, Khatmiyya leaders faced a major political dilemma. Because the brotherhood's adherents stretched across the tigre-shumagulle divide, they provided a valued but fragile religious continuity across Tigre-speaking society, which meant that its position on the issue could adversely affect its support among both segments of society. The BMA and many proactive shumagulle made a point of reaching out early to the al-Mirghani family in hopes of resolving the matter and dissuading activists from creating new "independent" clan structures. According to BMA officers, the Assab exiles associated with Tahgé who were responsible for promoting the idea of forming new clans also "went around collecting money from poor credulous people promising they won't have to pay and squandered the money collected on food and drink."[56]

In 1943, *sayyid* Jaᶜfar b. Bakri b. Jaᶜfar b. Muhammad ᶜUthman al-Mirghani died. He had been the head of the Khatmiyya's Eritrean branch and a longtime, politically astute intermediary for colonial authorities across the region. Following al-Mirghani's death and the continued growth of tigre dissatisfaction, BMA authorities turned to Jaᶜfar's nephew and heir apparent, *sayyid* Muhammad Abu Bakr al-Mirghani, for help. In February 1944, *sayyid* Muhammad made an eight-day tour of the ᶜAd Takles communities after being asked by officials in Keren to convince some of the rebellious sub-chiefs to pay their customary payments and withdraw support for the creation of new clan groups.[57] Although al-Mirghani reported

---

[55] *Trevaskis Papers,* Box 1 (b), "The Tigre-Speaking Peoples," 107.

[56] "Ad Takles Exiles, Assab ex. Keren," 1, BMA/DIS 260/kel 10957/66, RDC, Asmara.

[57] Despite his prestigious position in the brotherhood, *sayyid* Muhammad Abu Bakr Mirghani often received criticism for his apparent disinterest and idleness in local affairs. One British official noted in an intelligence report that only after he gave *sayyid* Muhammad

to British officials that most of the agitators had fled to the nearby mountains "rather than stay behind and be disrespectful" of his suggestions, he managed to procure a list of thirty activists allegedly responsible for inciting the local people to create their own clans.[58]

If the BMA and the shumagulle had reasoned that the al-Mirghani family's involvement would help bring most of the tigre activists to heel, they were only partially correct. While al-Mirghani successfully dissuaded most ʿAd Takles residents from establishing new clan structures, his visit also served to legitimize the basic aims of the emancipation movement. In a petition sent to Eritrea's Chief Administrator Darcy McCarthy in late March 1945, some tigre representatives recalled al-Mirghani's earlier visit and its significance to their cause:

> He noticed in person the condition of those virgin lands, covered with woods and stones, and the hard works which were taking place to make the ground tillable. As a result of such ascertainment, he stated to the BET ASGHEDE [*sic*] that his conscience did not allow him to bid the TIGRE [*sic*] to pay them [the shumagelle] a share of the crops, as it is unjust to sweat peoples, in opposition to Sciaria [*sic*] as well as to any human law.[59]

Consequently, much of the justification for serf emancipation stressed the dual violation of sharʾia law and basic human rights. Although *sayyid* Muhammad served as an intermediary between the shumagulle and the tigre, his limited support for their cause did not convince tigre emancipation leaders that the Khatmiyya leadership would back any radical change. Although al-Mirghani himself later took up the symbolic position of president of the largely pro-tigre Eritrean Muslim League in late 1946, the connection between the order's leadership and the tigre's grassroots movement proved inherently limited. *Sayyid* Muhammad al-Mirghani often came into direct conflict with the league's nonclerical administration and its overtly pro-tigre agenda; he eventually resigned from the organization in October 1949 and joined Eritrea's Unionist Party. Because a majority of

---

"a sound lecture" and had officials in Agordat speak directly with his father did he finally commit to speaking with the tigre communities. Major R. Signals, "Ad Tecles Tigre Dispute," 1, BMA/DIS 260/kel 10957/59, RDC, Asmara.

58 Major R. Signals, "Ad Tecles Disobedience," 1, BMA/DIS 260/kel 10957/42, RDC, Asmara.

59 "Untitled," 1, BMA/DIS 260/kel 10957/92, RDC, Asmara.

shumagulle also served in positions of leadership within the brotherhood and were often directly responsible for overseeing the payment of customary dues, Khatmiyya authorities as a whole did not sanction the tigre movement or provide its leaders with significant material support.

Thus, the movement's main actors, while recognizing the Khatmiyya order as the major regional Islamic authority, viewed their own identity as Muslims on different terms, especially with regard to broad ideas of social justice. Although much of the public justification from tigre representatives downplayed any inherent "Islamic" rationale for their activism, they nonetheless believed and articulated that their actions were part of a divinely ordained struggle for justice. One written appeal by tigre leaders explained that its constituency held a firm belief that "Italy was defeated because of God's punishment and because she did not protect our rights" as citizens from the injustices of the existing land tenure system.[60] As the momentum for tigre emancipation activity increased during the mid-1940s, activists became increasingly proactive in challenging the status quo on religious grounds, even if it meant risking the wrath of some Khatmiyya leaders. Tigre leaders across Eritrea's Western Province began preaching in public in the various villages and rural communities about how their condition represented an affront to God and the principles of justice defined within the Qur'an. Activists increasingly accused some Khatmiyya officials of ignoring Islamic teaching due to their failure to speak out on behalf of the tigre, especially those high-ranking *khalifas* and imams who came from shumagulle backgrounds. In some cases, tigre residents were forcibly removed from Friday prayers in Keren and Tessenei for allegedly discussing "tribal reorganization" with other worshipers prior to services. On some occasions, tigre activists even claimed that pro-shummagulle Khatmiyya officials openly encouraged communities to publicly shun those suspected of supporting emancipation or else they risked being excommunicated.[61] Thus, the split within religious discourse that emerged across the region reflected the social and class distinctions

[60] Ibid., 16.

[61] Eritrean Peoples Liberation Front, Central Administration of Eritrean Liberation, "A Questionnaire Regarding the Political Parties of the 1940s and 1950s," March 1, 1991. Ali Seʾid Bekhit Umar, interview, 01714 RDC, Asmara. Ironically, some Khatmiyya leaders also used similar tactics throughout early 1947 in trying to marginalize residents who did not initially support the Eritrean Muslim League. See *Trevaskis Papers,* Box 2 (a), *Four Power Commission of Investigation for the Former Italian Colonies,* Report on Eritrea, "Agordat 7th Dec. 1947," Appendix 143, 1–2.

already inherent to Tigre-speaking society. While the growing division in the dialogue stemmed in part from the already compromised position of Khatmiyya leadership within the al-Mirghani family, Muhammad al-Mirghani's own refusal to use his prominent position to directly address tigre concerns only encouraged the growing split. His support for relatively minimal gestures, such as temporarily easing some traditional customary payments, did not address the major positions taken by tigre activists, including the more substantial demands of ending the existing land tenure system and establishing new, "independent" clan units.

Many of the more secular-minded tigre activists appealed directly to British sympathies rather than channeling their arguments exclusively through religious language. Urban-based residents in particular actively submitted written appeals to administrators about how the legacy of both "divine and human laws" illustrated that the "residue of slavery" that had been imposed upon the tigre could only be wiped away if the British applied the appropriate "principles of Civilization and Liberty."[62] Tigre representatives carefully argued that their emancipation required not a broad rejection of all local (i.e., BMA) authority, but specifically freedom from the customary tributes and illegal taxes unknown to the presiding administration.[63] Moreover, tigre leaders often used their moralistic language and ideals to play on European sympathies as a means of garnering support. In describing the historical oppression of their status, they made a point of mentioning that their conditions were worse than slavery, "a form that not even the Nazis have given [the] world, while they are being accused of the ill treatment of humanity, humanity created partially by God, with all the organs of the body and the senses of man."[64]

The strategic language employed by activists also demonstrated that although the discontent among much of the population materialized as mass protest and refusal to pay, the responsibility for directing and articulating tigre appeals to colonial authorities fell to a small group of politically savvy merchants that had originally come up through the ranks of the previous Italian administration. Tigre representatives themselves alluded to this phenomenon, boasting that while the ranks of the shumagulle

---

[62] Ibid., 6.

[63] See "To H.E. Brigadier C. D'arcy Mc. Carthy O.B.E. Chief Administrator- Eritrea-Asmara," 15–20, BMA/DIS 260/kel 10957/89, RDC, Asmara.

[64] *Trevaskis Papers,* Box 2 (a), *Four Power Commission of Investigation for the Former Italian Colonies,* Report on Eritrea, "Letter of Tigré Representatives," Appendix 18, 2.

had fallen into a process of lethargy and "retrogression," the descents of many tigre "progressed enormously, passing from shepherds and cultivators to the arts, the free professions, commerce and employment both in government and commercial institutions."[65] Markakis also alluded to this professional imbalance between the two groups, stating that the tigre had "availed themselves of new employment opportunities in the colonial armies and police, raising their income, while also reducing the labour power available for herding their own and their masters' animals."[66] Of those tigre activists emerging from the "free professions," Ibrahim Sultan became the most influential and politically astute leader to articulate tigre concerns and the need to initiate dramatic reform across the region.

Ibrahim Sultan: The "Avocato" of Tigre Emancipation

In May 1945, a BMA intelligence report documented a general meeting of tigre and shumagulle that took place in the village of Sheddem the previous month. Of particular interest to authorities were the "irregularities" in the tigre arguments against making any future payments to the landlords. Authorities blamed the pointed and aggressive language of the tigre representatives on the influence of a meddling lawyer "whom the Tigre turned [to] for legal assistance." The man, referred to in the report as the "Avocato" (i.e., lawyer), could not be positively identified by either BMA or shumagulle observers. Nevertheless, the "Avocato" quickly gained a reputation as a "person who incites ignorant and gullible bushmen to disobey Government orders, who is afraid of putting his address on his letters and whose letters are falsely signed."[67] The descriptions of the individual in question perfectly fit that of Ibrahim Sultan and his specific contributions to the tigre cause.

Born to a tigre family from the Rugbat clan of the Beni-Amer and raised in Keren, Ibrahim Sultan embodied the climb of Eritrea's small Muslim professional class during Italian rule. Having received his initial Islamic education at a *khalwa* under the instruction of Jaᶜfar al-Mirghani, he later began his primary Arabic-language education as a student of

---

[65] Ibid., 5.

[66] Markakis, *National and Class Conflict in the Horn of Africa,* 59.

[67] Senior Civil Affairs Officer to B.M.A. Headquarters, "Ad Takles Tribe-Tigre/Shumagalle Dispute," 2, BMA/DIS 260/kel 10957/93, RDC, Asmara.

shaykh Osman Hasebela, himself a graduate of al-Azhar University.[68] As a youth, Sultan worked at a train depot in Agordat from 1922 to 1926. After being fired for allegedly engaging in an altercation with his Italian supervisor, he returned to Keren. Using his knowledge of Arabic, he procured a job in the colonial civil service as a translator and for the next several years traveled throughout Eritrea as part of the Italian colonial government's Native Affairs Department; his duties took him to many of the major towns and cities in western Eritrea, such as Agordat, Tessenei, and Addi Ugri (Mendefera), where he came into contact with other members of the relatively small indigenous civil service before deciding to practice law.[69] Sultan, like other members of the fledgling Muslim professional class, began linking with Islamic leaders across the colony, especially sympathetic authorities based in the major cities beyond tigre-dominated areas, including Asmara, Massawa, and Hirgigo.[70] Sultan and other activists formalized links between merchants and religious authorities by developing informal intellectual meeting groups, expanding charity organizations, and helping to establish new Islamic schools and mosques by the early 1940s. From these interactions emerged the core of what later became Eritrea's politically engaged Muslim intelligentsia.[71] In addition to simply concurring with their moral and religious justifications in criticizing treatment of the tigre, Sultan and his supporters found that many urban Muslim leaders also viewed emancipation as a major step toward helping establish a more unified, multiethnic, and politically active Muslim community across the country.

Sultan claimed that from an early age he had been instilled with a hatred for the injustices of the shumagulle. He recalled that he and his friends had been taunted as children and called "tiny worms" by their peers because of their serf origins. He also made a point of describing many of the most debasing kinds of treatment that shumagulle inflicted upon the tigre:

---

[68] Ibrahim Sultan, interview with Ahmed Haji Ali, Cairo, Egypt, March 20–25, 1982.

[69] Arefayne Bairu, "A Short History of Shaykh Ibrahim Sultan," 2–3, January 10, 1990, RDC, Asmara.

[70] Ibrahim Sultan, interview; Jamil Aman Mohammed, interview with author, Ottawa, Ontario, July 16, 2010; Yassin M. Aberra, "Muslim Institutions in Ethiopia: The Asmara Awqaf," *Journal of the Institute of Muslim Minority Affairs* 5, no. 1 (1984): 203–23.

[71] Most of these activists eventually formed the core of the Muslim membership within Mahber Fikri Hager (Party for the Love of Country), Eritrea's first indigenous, broad-based political organization formed during BMA rule. See Tesfai, *Aynfelale,* 33–36.

> When a Nabtab [shumagalle] child is born, before the umbilical cord is cut, one of the Tigres will be called and the cord is cut in front of him. The Tigre who was being called will thus be the slave of the child. The "bad-hair" of the child is never shaven without a Tigre being summoned; and the same thing for circumcision. The Tigre presented between the shaving and the circumcision would become the slaves of the child.[72]

Sultan took a passionate stand against the landowning aristocracy, denouncing their policies against the tigre as being both "un-Islamic" and a violation of basic human dignity. He contended publicly that their treatment was worse than slavery.[73] Moreover, his efforts at building a political constituency from among the disgruntled peasant groups followed the earlier efforts of some of the ʿAd Takles activists who had tried to create new clan structures while they also utilized their resources and connections as merchants to effect political change. For Trevaskis and most other BMA observers, the greatest irony about the surge in activism was the fact that it had primarily "been led and organised [*sic*] by the commercial class—composed of merchants in the towns and petty traders in the country."[74]

Although Trevaskis correctly observed the origins and economic strength of many of the movement's leaders, Sultan and his closest supporters had benefited not only from their financial standing but also from their experiences as low-level members of the "native" colonial administration, coming of age with a clear understanding about how the colonial system had appropriated the tigre-shumagelle divide. According to Sultan, Italian administrators long understood that "this kind of local traditional system would make the society highly fragmented and weak, and so the Italians encouraged the existing master-serf relationship among the Tigre society."[75] Idris Shubek, a tigre activist and an alleged relative of Tahgé, echoed this belief when he argued that the colonial appropriation and perversion of the traditional land system effectively created a "double

---

[72] Ibrahim Sultan, interview.

[73] Ibid.

[74] *Trevaskis Papers,* Box 1 (b), "The Tigre-Speaking Peoples," 116. In the midst of his political involvement Sultan owned and operated a cheese-processing plant in Tessenei from 1943 through 1945. See Woldeyesus Ammar, "Ibrahim Sultan Ali: A Liberator Who Passed Away 20 Years Ago Today," *Eritrean Human Rights Electronic Archive,* http://www.ehrea.org/Ibrahim0Sulta20Ali.pdf.

[75] Ibrahim Sultan, audio interview, Sudan, Audio-Visual Collection, RDC, Asmara.

slavery" for tigre living in servitude under both "native" and "colonial" authorities, which lasted until the BMA period.[76]

With Sultan's growing influence as both a legal and political organizer, and with discontent among the tigre communities reaching a boiling point by the summer of 1946, peasant representatives finally coalesced as a more cohesive political force. In August 1946, Ibrahim Sultan, along with Hamid Humed (one of Tahgé's confidents and fellow exiles in Assab) and colleague Imam Musa chaired a meeting of more than seven hundred tigre representatives in Sheddem. Unlike the previous meeting that had taken place in April 1945, the 1946 gathering, which excluded shumagulle representatives, explicitly laid out the basic objectives of the movement. Members passed a resolution nullifying their previous status as vassals and prohibited their brethren from milking animals or farming the land of the shumagulle. In addition, representatives also agreed to carry their program out into the rural areas to continue building support for the cause.[77] Throughout 1946, activists also benefited from the increased support of Muslim leaders in Asmara and Massawa, especially figures who wielded influence across both Muslim religious and economic life. Figures such as shaykh Abdelkadir Kebire, hajj Sulieman Ahmed Umar, *degiat* Hassan Ali, Saleh Kekiya Pasha, as well as the mufti provided institutional and, in some cases, direct financial support to Ibrahim Sultan's faction.[78]

By late November, other emerging issues began to influence the course of tigre emancipation. As arguments over Eritrea's political fate provoked factionalism across the colony, religious identity became increasingly politicized as most Muslim religious and community leaders began to formulate a pro-independence political movement. In early December, in response to the increased acrimony between Eritrea's pro-independence factions and those who supported union with neighboring Ethiopia, Ibrahim Sultan and a group of supporters that included several prominent members of Eritrea's urban-based Islamic clergy established the Eritrean

---

[76] Idris Shubek, audio interview, Agordat, Eritrea, 1988, Audio-Visual Collection, RDC, Asmara. Shubek claimed to be Tahgé's nephew.

[77] *Trevaskis Papers,* Box 2 (a), *Four Power Commission of Investigation for the Former Italian Colonies,* Report on Eritrea, "Letter of Tigré Representatives," Appendix 18, 8.

[78] See "This Is the Muslim League," *Sawt al-rabita al-islamiyya,* February 25, 1947, 2. *Degiat* represents an honorific military title, roughly translating as "Commander" or "General of the Gate." It is derived from the Amharic term *dejizmatch.*

Muslim League in Keren.[79] As the first nationalist organization within Eritrea, the league developed into a broad-based consortium that relied on the grassroots support of tigre members across the Western Province. Although the league initially included members of the al-Mirghani family and several influential shumagulle serving in symbolic leadership positions because of their continued importance as Islamic authorities, the organization's public embrace of emancipation, "tribal reorganization," and the aggressive antifeudal actions of its tigre-majority membership ultimately pushed most of the pro-shumagulle elements out of the league by mid-1947.[80] Sultan's position as the league's secretary general all but guaranteed that tigre emancipation would remain a key priority for the new organization. Consequently, tigre activism increasingly took on an enhanced role in the broader "national" dialogue, as tigre land reform represented one of the major issues that reverberated in discussions regarding Eritrean Muslims' overall political and economic well-being.

The Tigre Cause and the Eritrean Muslim League

What began as a series of localized opposition movements to the traditional land tenure system developed into a widespread movement for political power in Tigre-speaking areas of western and northern Eritrea. Under the leadership of activists such as Ibrahim Sultan, Mohamed Hamid Tahgé, Idris Faʾid, and others of "serf origins," Tigre-speaking peasants across the Western Province resisted in various ways against both shumagulle rule and the largely compromised BMA administration. Rejecting the above-mentioned parties' calls for more "moderate" solutions to their grievances,

[79] Although according to Ismael al-Mukhtar the mufti "was a very passionate nationalist, who was probably among the most knowledgeable on the intricacies of Eritrean politics," his position as the highest-ranking Islamic authority placed him in a delicate situation where his official duties did not allow him to take a public stance on political issues; consequently, he was absent at the league's first national conference in Keren in January 1947. He did, however, send his personal representative shaykh Idris Hussein Suleiman to give the league his blessing and included a letter of support. Ismael al-Mukhtar, interview.

[80] Ironically, the league leadership's first official meeting took place within the residence of the late *sayyid* Jaʿfar al-Mirghani. See *Trevaskis Papers,* Box 2 (a), *Four Power Commission of Investigation for the Former Italian Colonies,* Report on Eritrea, "Council of Foreign Ministers (Deputies): Two Chiefs of the Western Province," Appendix 128, 2; "Moslem League, Eritrea," Appendix 107, 3.

the peasant leaders saw themselves engaged in nothing short of a struggle to end the "continuous state of slavery" within tigre society.[81] Indeed, as the later political ramifications of their movement demonstrate, tigre activists emerged with a profound understanding of their own "negation" as a subject class whose existence under shumagulle control remained the preferred system of governance not only for local landlords but for both Italian and British authorities as a means to maintain control across the region.[82]

The eventual establishment of the Eritrean Muslim League in Keren in November 1946 demonstrated nationalists' investment in what Jordan Gebre-Medhin called the "new confidence of the serfs" and the growing political cohesion among Muslims as a whole.[83] That said, activists' decision to name their organization the Eritrean Muslim League also demonstrated how the leadership within its Executive Council attempted to fuse the quest for political independence with a genuine interest in how Islamic institutions and religious thought more broadly could serve the public. The league's name was also a tribute to the All-India Muslim League, and reflected Eritrean Muslim intellectuals' global awareness of the broader nationalist trends occurring across the Islamic world.[84] The decision to establish an explicitly "Muslim" political party also revealed that several factions within the organization expressed varying ideas about whose "interests" the league would ultimately serve.

Indeed, the league leadership struggled throughout its first two years to balance support from traditional elites, such as the al-Mirghani family and the various clan chiefs, with the organization's close links to tigre activism. Other factions, including most of the merchant communities in Asmara and Massawa, viewed the league as a vehicle to focus on urban renewal and institutional investment within Muslim communities on the national level. Not surprisingly, the league's founding conference concluded with a series of public resolutions that did not address policies

---

[81] *Trevaskis Papers,* Box 2 (a), *Four Power Commission of Investigation for the Former Italian Colonies,* Report on Eritrea, "Letter of Tigré Representatives," Appendix 18, 1.

[82] Ranajit Guha, *Elementary Aspects of Peasant Insurgency in Colonial India* (Delhi: Oxford University Press, 1983), 18.

[83] Jordan Gebre-Medhin, *Peasants and Nationalism in Eritrea: A Critique of Ethiopian Studies* (Trenton: Red Sea Press, 1989), 152.

[84] Redie Bereketeab, *Eritrea: The Making of a Nation, 1890–1991* (Trenton: Red Sea Press, 2007), 270.

aimed at placating one specific subgroup, but instead embraced several broad points relating to complete Eritrean independence.[85] Nevertheless, a growing number of tigre members became the driving force that steered Ibrahim Sultan and other league leaders in a more openly grassroots direction by mid-1947. The emphasis on empowering those most oppressed within traditional social structures across the colony was not lost on either league leaders or BMA authorities as the nationalist movement widened. In July 1947, Trevaskis reflected on the league's surge of grassroots popularity in connection to the tigre issue:

> I made the mistake of expecting political leadership, if it came at all, to come from the chiefs. In fact it came in the first instance from the huge mass of serf or subject classes which remain in a state of political & partial economic subjugation to the small aristocratic ruling groups of the Northern & Western Eritrean tribes.[86]

Indeed, at almost the exact same time, the Muslim League was established, and Ibrahim Sultan gained his broadest support for tigre emancipation and British intervention in the much-discussed clan restructuring.[87] According to Gaim Kibreab, Sultan and his supporters' later success in working with the BMA and the shumagulle could not have been achieved without the legacy of the "deeply embedded social organization that was inherited from the past" and the subsequent contributions of many sympathetic members of the Muslim clergy who helped to resolve conflicts.[88] Indeed, this inheritance was linked with the considerable activism of Muslim authorities among the tigre; Ibrahim Sultan's colleagues in cities such as Keren and Agordat used their religious authority—much as Muslim businessmen used their economic influence—to shape the negotiations with

---

[85] "This Is the Muslim League," *Sawt al-rabita al-islamiyya,* February 25, 1947, 2. See *Nay Ertra Semunawi Gazzetta,* March 5, 1947, 1; Tesfai, *Aynfelale,* 199.

[86] Fabian Colonial Bureau, Bodleian Library, Oxford University, MSS Brit. Emp., s 365, 180/3. Kennedy Trevaskis to Dr. Rita Hinden, July 24, 1947, 3–4.

[87] See Jan-Bart Gewald, "Making Tribes: Social Engineering in the Western Province of British-Administered Eritrea, 1941–1952," *Journal of Colonialism and Colonial History* 2 (Winter 2000); FO 1015/138, "A Report on Tribal Reorganization in the Western Province," 1–34.

[88] Gaim Kibreab, *Critical Reflections on the Eritrean War of Independence: Social Capital, Associational Life, Religion, Ethnicity and Sowing the Seeds of Dictatorship* (Trenton: Red Sea Press, 2008), 88.

BMA officials and quell the uprisings.[89] As the Muslim League emerged in early 1947 as the largest and most influential nationalist organization in Eritrea, its agenda and most of the key personnel within its administration had made tigre emancipation a key platform. Even the Muslim League's official Arabic newspaper, *Sawt al-Rabita* (*Voice of the League*), included ongoing coverage of the tigre issue and several commentaries about the need to procure freedom for tigre communities.[90]

Thus, the tigre rebellions—exemplified by both the physical actions against the shumagulle and the written appeals of representatives—gave rise to a newfound identity among the Tigre-speaking peoples, in which local people were empowered to displace the old colonial-backed system with new social structures to shape their destiny. At a broader level, tigre representatives illustrated by the middle of the decade how the Muslim masses in Eritrea could serve as a politically viable force beyond the issue of serf emancipation. This rise in tigre-peasant activism against the traditional systems of authority dovetailed with the growing politicization of religion taking place across the country. Although it presaged the development of formal nationalist political parties by several years, the tigre emancipation movement demonstrated at least three key features that would later define the core intellectual preoccupations among Eritrea's predominantly pro-independence Muslim activists. Broad ideas about the need for grassroots participation to address injustice, the use of Islamic teaching as a means of social and economic liberation, and the rise of a small, proactive Muslim intelligentsia within the leadership apparatus all signified how early tigre mobilization helped concretize ideas about religious identity, political representation, and the nature of community within a genuine "Eritrean" context.

[89] Trevaskis, "Report on Serfdom," 1, FO 230/255, June 5, 1948; Ibrahim Sultan, interview.
[90] See "This Is the Muslim League," *Sawt al-rabita al-islamiyya,* February 25, 1947, 2; "We and Independence," *Sawt al-rabita al-islamiyya,* March 4, 1947, 1; "There Is Nothing More Preferable to the Muslim Than Dying for the Truth," *Sawt al-rabita al-islamiyya,* December 23, 1947, 1; Ahmed Muhammad Ibrahim al-Tigrawi, "Feudal System," *Sawt al-rabita al-islamiyya,* December 9, 1949, 1.

SOURCES

Central Sudanic Arabic Scripts (Part 2): *Barnāwī**

Andrea Brigaglia, UNIVERSITY OF CAPE TOWN
Mauro Nobili, UNIVERSITY OF CAPE TOWN

DOI: 10.5192/215409930402195

ABSTRACT

This article describes and analyzes barnāwī, the Arabic script of Borno (northeastern Nigeria) and most ancient prototype of what we define as the Central Sudanic family of scripts. Barnāwī *shows paleographic features that clearly set it apart from some other West African Arabic scripts, thereby confirming the inadequacy of the label sūdānī, which often surfaces in literature to collectively brand a variety of scripts used in different regions of West Africa. A paleographic analysis of barnāwī also suggests that its origins predate the development of the maghribī script in North Africa in the twelfth century.*

*This article has gone through a long process of gestation. The idea was conceived in 2007 thanks to the important comments that Muhammad Sani Umar made after Andrea Brigaglia's presentation on the calligraphers of Kano at the second international European Conference of African Studies (ECAS 2) in Leiden. After several revisions, that paper developed into the first installment of the present article, which appeared in an earlier issue of this journal (Andrea Brigaglia, "Central Sudanic Arabic Scripts (Part 1): The Popularization of the Kanawī Script," *Islamic Africa* 2, no. 2 [2011]: 51–85). The idea was revived again in June 2010 when Andrea Brigaglia and Mauro Nobili found themselves discussing the paleographic features of the scripts found in the images of dozens of manuscripts from the de Gironcourt collection of West African manuscripts, all of which were spread out in front of them on an overcrowded desk in a room in Naples. Mauro Nobili eventually developed this discussion into a wider project on West African scripts, some of the results of which have already appeared in an earlier issue of this journal (Mauro Nobili, "Arabic Scripts in West African Manuscripts: A Tentative Classification from the de Gironcourt Manuscript Collec-

Islamic Africa, VOL. 4, NO. 2, 2013. ISSN 2154-0993.

Introduction

In recent issues of this journal, the authors published two articles addressing from different angles the Arabic scripts and calligraphies displayed in West African manuscripts.[1] Mauro Nobili highlighted how the category "Sudanic" (*sūdānī*) is often applied uncritically to a number of different scripts used in the southern Sahara and sub-Saharan regions known in Arabic literature as the *bilād al-Sūdān.*[2] According to Nobili, these scripts have little in common, both in paleographic features and in their historical development.[3] Andrea Brigaglia, on the other hand, identified a peculiar calligraphy that became popular in the twentieth century in the northern Nigerian city of Kano. This calligraphic style, called *kanawī,* developed from an earlier model, henceforth called *barnāwī,* which is the script of Borno, an area composed of northeastern Nigeria and southwestern Chad. In both papers, the term "Central Sudanic" is used to refer to a script tradition that displays a number of common features that set it aside from the rest of the West African scripts.[4]

---

tion," *Islamic Africa* 2, no. 1 [2011]: 105–33). In 2012, Mauro Nobili was granted a University Research Committee postdoctoral fellowship at the University of Cape Town, and the two authors found the chance to sit together and develop their thoughts into a coherent piece. The article has also benefited from the precious comments of Dmitry Bondarev and François Déroche, both of whom the authors warmly thank for their (occasionally critical, but always encouraging) insights. The comments of the two anonymous reviewers of an earlier draft have contributed to make the article more readable and our argument clearer. A final acknowledgment goes to Abdulaleem Somers for his kind proofreading.

[1] The term "script" refers to a set of distinctive and recurring paleographic features learned spontaneously in the process of acquiring basic writing skills and often used unconsciously. The term "calligraphy," by contrast, refers to a style of writing that is intended to be decorative. A given script can always be realized in calligraphic and noncalligraphic fashions.

[2] Although *sūdānī* has the advantage of explicitly referring to the geographic area where these scripts are used, the authors of the present article believe that the term is inadequate, even as a generic umbrella, to collectively describe the variety of scripts of different origins and separate development found in the region in question.

[3] Nobili, "Arabic Scripts in West African Manuscripts."

[4] Brigaglia, "Central Sudanic Arabic Scripts (Part 1)," A detail of that article needs to be corrected: Sharīf Bala Gabari and Sharīf Bala Zaitawa, identified in the article as two signatures of the same calligrapher, are in fact the names of two different calligraphers of Kano. The identification made in the article of Sharīf Bala Gabari as the first self-conscious calligraphic artist of Kano, however, has been confirmed by a recent research trip (January 2012) in which the author has observed one of the students of the master calligrapher, Muḥammad al-Sādis Yūsuf, producing posters of calligraphic realizations of popular prayers or verses

Starting from a critical review of the literature on West African Arabic scripts, this article will emphasize how most of the extant literature implicitly refers to the tradition of Borno as the most peculiar script employed in West Africa. Yet, most contributors have mistakenly identified the Borno tradition as representative of the whole region and considered it as a late offshoot of the *maghribī* script, leading to the emergence of the nebulous category of *sūdānī*. The authors of the present article, on the contrary, believe in the existence of different and internally consistent scripts employed in various geographic areas of West Africa. Among these, the Central Sudanic should be considered as an ancient family of scripts that developed parallel to the *maghribī*, but independently from it. Our choice of "Central Sudanic" follows the geographical taxonomy employed in the seminal series led by John O. Hunwick, *The Arabic Literature of Africa*. Its second volume, entitled *The Writings of Central Sudanic Africa*, is devoted to an area encompassing "the Federal Republic of Nigeria, [. . . and] the present republics of Chad, Cameroun and Niger," which is the host region of the script here discussed.[5]

After a critical analysis of the extant literature on *sūdānī*, the article will move to an analysis of the most ancient subtype of Central Sudanic—i.e., the above-mentioned Borno tradition (*barnāwī*).[6] Our analysis will consist of a description of the paleographic features of *barnāwī* and a discussion of its historical origins. By linking *barnāwī* to the early developments of the Arabic scripts in North Africa and the Middle East, this contribution will also question the stereotype that West African script traditions are a late offshoot of the *maghribī*.

---

of the Qur'an in the typical style of his teacher. As this seems to be the first example of this type, it confirms the role of Sharīf Bala Gabari in mediating a wider transition from a traditional scribal culture to a calligraphic one.

[5] John O. Hunwick et al., *Arabic Literature of Africa II: The Writings of Central Sudanic Africa* (Leiden: Brill, 1995).

[6] Borno has probably witnessed a development of Islamic culture and literacy since the eleventh century. The Islamic tradition of Borno had a heavy influence in the central Saharan and Sahelian region. The most useful contributions to the history of Islam in precolonial Borno are two theses: Abubakar Mustapha, "The Contribution of the Sayfawa *ʿUlamāʾ* to the Study of Islam c. 1086–1846 AD" (Ph.D. diss., Kano, Bayero University, 1987), and Hamidu Bobboyi, "The *ʿUlamāʾ* of Borno: A Study of the Relations Between Scholars and State Under the Sayfawa, 1470–1808" (Ph.D. diss., Evanston, Ill., Northwestern University, 1992). For a general overview of the history of Islam in Borno, see John E. Lavers, "Islam in the Bornu Caliphate," *Odu: A Journal of West African Studies* 5 (1971): 27–53.

The Theory of Sūdānī

In the literature on Arabic calligraphy, the category *sūdānī* frequently surfaces in reference to the West African script(s). *Sūdānī* is usually presented as an all-inclusive category for the whole region and is discussed in the wider framework of so-called *maghribī.*[7]

The first scholar to introduce the category *sūdānī* was Octave V. Houdas who, in an 1886 article, identified four variants of the *maghribī* tradition.[8] After discussing *andalusī, fāsī,* and *qayrawānī,* Houdas briefly described *sūdānī* as follows:

> The coarse outlook of the *soudany* [*sic*] makes it easy to recognize. The heavy shapes of the letters are extremely irregular; the stroke is alternatively thick and thin. The vertical stems are highly elevated, disproportionately with the thickness of the script and the shapes of the curves. The overall inclination of the script is strongly accentuated and bends toward the left. Without this inclination, the general outlook would be that of a coarse Kufic traced by a hesitant hand.[9]

Addressing the issue of the origins of *sūdānī,* Houdas suggested—albeit cautiously—that it might have developed in Timbuktu.[10] This hypothesis is not grounded in firm historical evidence, as Houdas himself admitted, but it reflects the author's overall assumption that any important development in the intellectual history of Islam is rooted in an urban milieu.[11] With Houdas's article, the two "cornerstones" of the theory of *sūdānī* are established: (1) the existence of one regional script used across

---

[7] See, for example, David James, *Qur'ans and Bindings from the Chester Beatty Library: A Facsimile Exhibition* (London: World of Islam Festival Trust, 1980), 117 (the manuscript is described as item no. 95; however, the facsimile is misplaced at p. 116, in place of item no. 94); Marianna S. Simpson, "A Manuscript of the Qur'an from Sub-Saharan Africa (W. 853)," *Journal of the Walters Art Museum* 62 (2004): 237–38.

[8] Octave V. Houdas, "Essai sur l'écriture maghrébine," *Publications de l'École des Langues Orientales Vivantes* 19 (1886): 85–115.

[9] Ibid., 109–10 (our translation).

[10] Ibid., 104. The assumption that so-called *sūdānī* was generated in Timbuktu resurfaces sometimes in the literature; see, for example, Galla Dicko et al., "Trésors écrits du centre Ahmed Baba de Tombouctou," in *Les bibliothèques du désert: Recherches et études sur un millénaire d'écrits,* ed. Attilio Gaudio (Paris: L'Harmattan, 2002), 222.

[11] The pivotal role of the city in the development of Islamic culture is a peculiar trope of the Orientalist tradition (Jean-Louis Triaud, "L'Islam nell'Africa Occidentale: Una storia urbana di lungo periodo," in *Islam e città nell'Africa a sud del Shahara: Tra sufismo e fondamentalismo,* ed. Adriana Piga [Naples: Liguori, 2001], 132).

West Africa; (2) this script is considered a rudimentary subcategory of *maghribī* displaying many characteristics of so-called "Kufic."[12]

The theory of *sūdānī* was further developed by Nabia Abbott in the 1930s.[13] In her article on a West African handwritten copy of the Qurʾan, Abbott devoted a short section to an analysis of its hand, which she described as "the widespread Sudanese variety of the Maghribī script" and "a combination of the old angular Kufic and of modern cursive forms."[14] Although here the paleographic description of some of the letters is very accurate, Abbott's article still suffers from the uncritical use of the category *sūdānī* for the whole West African region. Moreover, Houdas's assumption that *sūdānī* represents a rudimentary and unpolished style is further amplified and infused with racial prejudices by Abbott: "the general appearance [of the script] is coarse and heavy" and it "shows in its primitiveness sufficient similarity to the so-called arts of Central and West Africa."[15]

Although some scholars have since questioned the validity of *sūdānī* as an analytic category (as detailed below), this term has gained strength in some very influential publications since the late 1990s. In a volume of the well-known series *Nasser D. Khalili Collection of Islamic Art,* Tim Stanley reproposes the notion that there is one script "used throughout Western Sudan," which is "a member of the Maghribi group."[16] A few years later, the theory of *sūdānī* reached its full expression with Sheila S. Blair's well-known 2006 book on Islamic calligraphy, as well as with her subsequent essay "Arabic Calligraphy in West Africa."[17]

---

[12] In the last few years, scholars of Arabic paleography have increasingly avoided the long-established term "Kufic," since the latter is often applied to different scripts having but a few characteristics in common (see, for example, François Déroche et al., "Islamic Codicology: An Introduction to the Study of Manuscripts in Arabic Script" [London: Al-Furqan Islamic Heritage Foundation, 2006], 216). The authors of the present paper have decided to maintain the term only when referring to secondary literature where the term appears.

[13] Nabia Abbott, "Maghribī Koran Manuscripts of the Seventeenth to the Eighteenth Centuries," *American Journal of Semitic Languages and Literatures* 55, no. 1 (1938): 61–65.

[14] Ibid., 63.

[15] Ibid. These kinds of unacceptable judgments are reproduced in more recent scholarship. For example, in a well-known exhibition of manuscripts from the Chester Beatty Library, David James refers to "a rather primitive type used in West Africa called *Sūdānī*" (James, *Qurʾans and Bindings,* 109).

[16] Tim Stanley, "The Qurʾanic Script of Western Sudan: Maghribi or Ifriqi," in *The Nasser D. Khalili Collection of Islamic Art, Vol. IV, The Decorated Word: Qurʾans of the 17th to 19th Centuries AD, Part One,* by Manijfeh Bayani, Tim Stanley, and Anna Contadini (New York: Nour Foundation, in association with Azimuth Editions and Oxford University Press, 1998), 34.

[17] Sheila S. Blair, *Islamic Calligraphy* (Edinburgh: Edinburgh University Press, 2006), 571–75; and Sheila S. Blair, "Arabic Calligraphy in West Africa," in *The Meanings of Timbuktu,*

Although Blair expresses some reservations about the terminology and avoids *sūdānī* only because it may lead to confusion with the modern state of Sudan,[18] she ends up reproposing the same theory in another disguise through her use of the overall term "West African script." Reproducing Houdas's hypothesis, Blair assumes that there exists an "ideal" Arabic script used throughout West Africa.[19] Without substantiating her claim with convincing paleographic evidence, she also asserts that the West African script/*sūdānī* "clearly derives from the Maghribi."[20]

Blair's basic assumption that the West African script/*sūdānī* derives from the *maghribī* family is not convincing, as we will explain below. However, this is already evident in the very pictures of two handwritten copies of the Quran from Borno published in earlier secondary literature and reproduced in Blair's paper, as well as in other published images of Arabic manuscripts from the same area.[21] Several features that Blair herself identifies as typical of "all four subtypes of Maghribi script,"[22] in fact, are absent from most of these Bornuan manuscripts. Among these are the possibility for a single letter to "assume four or five different shapes on the same page"; ascenders for *alif, lām,* and *ṭāʾ/ẓāʾ* being "curved, not rigidly straight" and having "a large dot or serif that faces left"; and exaggerated "ends of the letters, especially *sin, sad, lam, mim* and *nun.*"[23] On the contrary, other features identified by Blair as typical of *maghribī* are also found in Bornuan manuscripts; namely, a connected final *alif* descending below the baseline, and the bodies of *ṣād* and *ṭāʾ/ẓāʾ* being elliptical and smooth, lacking the final notch.

Likewise and conversely, some of the features identified by Blair as typical of Borno Qurʾānic manuscripts' hands—namely, squat letters on a flat baseline, and equal height of the letters[24]—are not typical of the

ed. Shamil Jeppie and Souleymane B. Diagne (Cape Town: Human Sciences Research Council, 2008), 59–75.

[18] Blair, "Arabic Calligraphy in West Africa," 61.

[19] Ibid., 60, 61, 71, and 72.

[20] Ibid., 66.

[21] See, for example, Qurʾanic and non-Qurʾanic manuscripts described in Adrian D. H. Bivar, "A Dated Kuran from Bornu," *Nigeria Magazine* 65 (1960): 199–205; and Adrian D. H. Bivar, "Arabic Documents of Northern Nigeria," *Bulletin of the School of Oriental and African Studies* 22, nos. 1–3 (1959): 324–49.

[22] Blair, "Arabic Calligraphy in West Africa," 61.

[23] These appear in Blair, "Arabic Calligraphy in West Africa," 60.

[24] Ibid., 62.

maghribī tradition as a whole. This can be clearly observed in the pictures of *maghribī* manuscripts displayed in her article.[25]

Furthermore, Blair's historical outline of the development of Arabic writing culture in the region, which provides the basis for her hypothesis about the origins of this script, is fundamentally flawed. Blair's hypothesis is that the West African script/*sūdānī* is a later offshoot that has developed out of *maghribī* in a relatively recent time (between the sixteenth and the eighteenth centuries). Her assumption is that from the eleventh to the fifteenth century, Arabic manuscripts were *read* but not *produced* in West Africa: "Production may have begun as early as the sixteenth century, and increased gradually in the seventeenth century . . . [However,] Arabic manuscripts became common in the eighteenth and nineteenth centuries such as we can talk of a distinct West African style of script."[26]

Even granting that her chronology is accurate, the shortage of manuscript books cannot be taken as proof of the absence of a culture of writing. The seminal study of Paulo de Moraes Farias on inscriptions on tombstones and steles proves the presence of a culture of writing in the Arabic alphabet in West Africa starting from the early eleventh century.[27] Arabic sources testify to diplomatic exchanges between the courts of sub-Saharan states, also starting from the eleventh century.[28] Moreover, the Qurʾan was probably studied in West Africa since the early first millennium CE. Until recently, the primary support of elementary Qurʾanic learning was the wooden slate (*lawḥ*), where the verses of the Qurʾan were continuously written, studied, and washed off. Attendance of the Qurʾanic school was an essential part of the socialization of a Muslim child, and basic Arabic writing skills have been transmitted on a large scale through this institution for centuries.[29] This is true not only for West Africa, but also for the

[25] Ibid., 67–68.

[26] Ibid., 69–70.

[27] Paulo de Moraes Farias, *Arabic Medieval Inscriptions from the Republic of Mali* (Oxford: Oxford University Press, 2003).

[28] An epistolary exchange is attested at the end of the eleventh century between an unnamed ruler of the empire of Ghana and the Almoravid emir Yūsuf b. Tashfīn (d. 500/1106) in the anonymous *Kitāb al-istibṣār* (see Nehemia Levtzion and J. F. K Hopkins, *Corpus of Early Arabic Sources for West African History* [Princeton, N.J.: Marcus Wiener, 2000], 146).

[29] See, for example, Ibn Baṭṭūṭa, who reports that the people of some cities of the empire of Mali were particularly devoted to teaching their children the memorization of the Qurʾan (see Levtzion and Hopkins, *Corpus of Early Arabic Sources,* 285). In Borno, the foundation of a system of Qurʾanic studies is traced by oral sources back to the eleventh century

wider Muslim world in premodern times, when paper was never a common support for elementary education. In other words, the transmission of the basic features of a given script in a given region used to take place before a student had access to manuscript books on paper support, which was reserved only for more advanced students. (See figure 1.)

Furthermore, the absence of surviving manuscripts that predate the eighteenth and nineteenth centuries cannot be taken as evidence of the absence of manuscripts in earlier dates. In these regards, Constant Hamès's valuable remark that the scarcity of West African manuscripts of ancient date is to be related to the precarious conditions of conservation in the region[30] is complemented by Bruce Hall and Charles S. Stewart's observation that paper produced before the eighteenth century had in West Africa a life span of only about 150–200 years, making it necessary to recopy a work at least every two centuries.[31] To conclude, the shortage of manuscripts dating back prior to the eighteenth century does not justify the claim that West Africa did not develop distinctive scripts until that date.

The following section of this article will show that a more careful study of the scripts displayed in the manuscripts from the region reveals the existence in West Africa of a variety of styles of different origins.

Recognizing the Existence of Different Scripts

Although the theory of *sūdānī* remains the dominant paradigm in the studies on West African Arabic manuscripts, some scholars have challenged the assumption that the region is characterized by a uniform style.

A recent contribution by Hamès, focusing on Qurʾanic manuscripts from different areas of West Africa, convincingly shows the existence of

(Mustapha, *The Contribution of the Sayfawa ʿUlamāʾ,* 109) and derived from a Qayrawān (Tunisia) model (ibid., 118). In the late twelfth century, the region of Borno produced a grammarian and poet (Ibrāhīm b. Yaʿqub al-Kānemī) who, educated in local circles of learning, ended up teaching in Morocco and died in Andalusia (Hunwick, *Arabic Literature of Africa II,* 17–19).

[30] Constant Hamès, "Les manuscrits arabo-africains: Des particularités?" *Revue des Mondes Musulmans et de la Méditerranée* 99–100 (2002), special issue, "La tradition manuscrite en écriture arabe," ed. Geneviève Humbert, 174–75.

[31] Bruce Hall and Charles S. Stewart, "The Historic 'Core Curriculum' and the Book Market in Islamic West Africa," in *The Trans-Saharan Book Trade: Manuscript Culture, Arabic Literacy and Intellectual History in Muslim Africa,* ed. Graziano Krätli and Ghislaine Lydon (Leiden: Brill, 2011), 149.

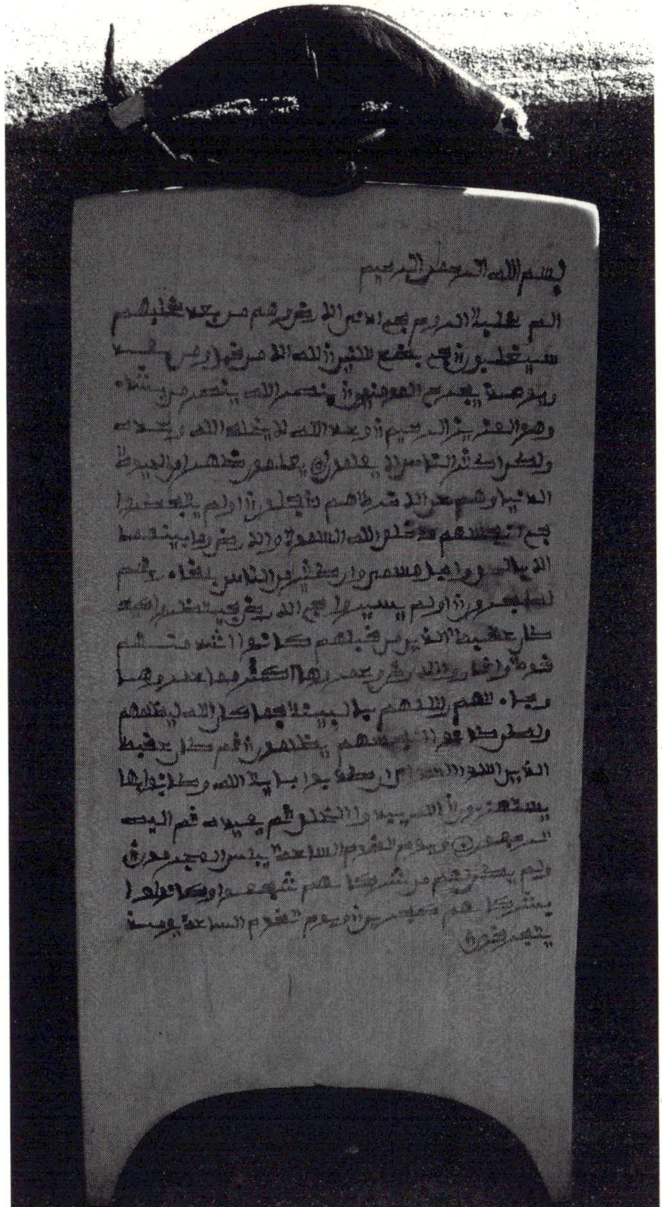

Figure 1. A wooden board (*lawḥ*) of a Qurʾan student trained in Borno. Photo courtesy of Andrea Brigaglia.

different types of script in the region.[32] By comparing two Mauritanian, a Chadian, and a "West African" copy of the Qurʾan, Hamès proposes that there exists no such thing as an overall *sūdānī* subtype of *maghribī,* but that different scripts have evolved separately in the region. Such a conclusion is substantiated by an exceptional wealth of evidence, in both the images provided and the meticulous descriptions of the scripts.[33] Moreover, this contribution identifies a separate type of script peculiar to Mauritania and the western Sahara, which is so close to *maghribī* that one even wonders about "its eventual distinction" or, alternately, "its complete integration" into *maghribī.*[34]

Less convincing, on the other hand, is Hamès's interpretation of the scripts of the West African Qurʾan of unknown origin and of the "Chadian" one.[35] The Qurʾan that Hamès dubs as West African is in fact treated as representative of the Borno tradition, the diffusion of which is arbitrarily extended to the whole West African region.[36] However, the script of this copy of the Qurʾan does not match closely any of the well-known examples of Bornuan script. On the other hand, the script that Hamès calls Chadian—and which he believes was strongly influenced by the scripts of the Fezzan and Egypt—is a typical example of the Qurʾanic scribal tradition of Borno, whose influence certainly extends well into the contemporary state of Chad but is not limited to it.[37]

---

[32] Constant Hamès, "Corans africains manuscripts: Vers une typologie," in *Le temps des Oulèmas: Les manuscripts africains comme sources historique,* ed. Seyni Moumouni and Viera Pawlikova-Vilhanova (Niamey: Université Abdou Moumouni de Niamey et Union Académique Internationale, 2009), 29–57.

[33] The hand of the first copy of the Qurʾan from Mauritania is just defined as an "ordinary hand" (Hamès, "Corans africains," 46); the hand of the second is described at pp. 48–49; the "Chadian" copy is at pp. 50–51; finally, the "West African" copy is at pp. 53–54.

[34] Hamès, "Corans africains," 55.

[35] For illustrations of both, see Hamès, "Corans africains," respectively at pp. 64–66 and 61–63.

[36] Hamès, "Corans africains," 55.

[37] The precise geographic extension of the Central Sudanic script tradition must still be demarcated. During a sojourn in N'Djamena in 2009, one of the authors of the present article was shown a copy of the Qurʾan, reportedly written in Wadai (eastern Chad) about 200 years ago, and closely resembling the Bornuan model. This copy is the private possession of Sīdī Hamza al-Sanūsī, a Qurʾanic teacher of Maba origin from Abéché (Wadai). Islam in Wadai has developed in close connections with Darfur. This area can be considered as the meeting point of an "eastern" (*mashriqī*) and a western (*maghribī*) Islamic tradition in Africa (Rüdiger Seesemann, "Where East Meets West: Islamic Educational Institutions in Darfur/

To sum up, Hamès's contribution is crucial inasmuch as it clearly shows—via a comparative analysis of scripts from different areas of West Africa—the limits of the assumption that one Arabic script is used in the entire region. Nevertheless, the taxonomy he proposes is not fully satisfactory.

Another tentative taxonomy is the one employed by the team of scholars who are cataloging some collections of Timbuktu under the auspices of the al-Furqan Islamic Heritage Foundation.[38] In these publications, the different scripts of the Timbuktu manuscripts are classified as *maghribī, ṣaḥrāwī, sūqī,* and *sūdānī.* Unfortunately, these scholars do not explain their criteria for such classification. An exception is represented by some brief but important observations in an unpublished paper in Arabic by the Timbuktu researcher and calligrapher Maḥmūd Dadab, known as Ḥammū,[39] as well as in a very brief note in a paper by Galla Dicko on the manuscripts of the Institut des Hautes Études et de Recherches Islamiques Ahmed Baba (formerly Centre de Documentation et de Recherches Ahmed Baba).[40] However, in neither of these cases is the taxonomy supplemented with a satisfactory description of the scripts, and the absence of any image associated with the four categories precludes any outsider from benefiting from it. Another problem associated with the above taxonomy is that it suffers what might be called "Timbuktu-centrism." The scripts used in the Sahelo-Saharan area around Timbuktu (*maghribī, ṣaḥrāwī,* and *sūqī*) are in fact well analyzed, while the resurfacing label *sūdānī* is used as an overall category for the rest of West Africa, which is geographically and culturally distant from Timbuktu.[41]

More recently, the consistency of the category *sūdānī* has been radically called into question by Nobili. Basing his study on the scripts of a number of dated and situated manuscripts from the de Gironcourt

Sudan," *Islam et Sociétés au Sud du Sahara* 13 [1999]: 41–61). We do not know, however, if the Central Sudanic ever became the dominant script in the area or if, on the contrary, its influence was only limited to the groups that had a direct historical, ethnic, and political link with the Kanuri of western Chad and northern Nigeria.

[38] The first catalog in which this taxonomy is employed is Sidi Amar Ould Ely et al., *Handlist of Manuscripts in the Centre de Documentation et de Recherches Historiques Ahmad Baba, Timbuktu, Mali,* 5 vols. (London: al-Furqan Islamic Heritage Foundation, 1995–1998).

[39] Maḥmūd Muḥammad Dadab [*al-mulaqqab* Ḥammū], *Al-Makhṭūṭāt al-ʿarabiyya wa-l-maktūba bi-l-ḥarf al-ʿarabī fī minṭaqat al-sāḥil al-ifrīqī* (n.p.), 16–17.

[40] Galla Dicko et al., "Trésor écrits," 22.

[41] Nobili, "Arabic Scripts in West African Manuscripts," 115.

collection,[42] Nobili has further developed the taxonomy employed by the Timbuktu scholars. In two articles dedicated to West African scripts, Nobili accepts the existence of *sūqī* and *ṣaḥrāwī* as two distinct scripts, and describes their respective paleographic features. He also suggests that a third script with markedly distinctive traits—which he calls Central Sudanic cursive hands—is used in the area of the Central Sudan and that it developed from the scribal tradition of Borno.[43]

In the first installment of this article, Brigaglia discusses the *kanawī,* a Nigerian calligraphic style popularized in twentieth-century religious literature produced mainly in Kano. As in the case of Nobili's Central Sudanic cursive hands, Brigaglia also suggests that *kanawī* should not be considered as a script of its own, but as a variant of the old script tradition of neighboring Borno, whose influence extends throughout the Central Sudan.[44]

Borno, we argue, is the cradle of a script that is diffused in an area encompassing the modern states of Cameroon, Chad, Niger, and Nigeria. We thus refer to it as *barnāwī* and treat it as the archetypal subtype of the larger script family we have dubbed Central Sudanic. *Barnāwī* displays a marked paleographic uniformity, as a quick look at the manuscripts from Nigeria and Chad reproduced in Abbott, James, Simpson, Blair, and Hamès reveals.[45] *Barnāwī* is attested since at least the mid-seventeenth century, and is still employed in the same way today in the Qurʾanic schools of the area and in the many handwritten copies of the Qurʾan that are produced by the students who specialize in Qurʾanic memorization, orthography, and calligraphy.[46]

Convinced that only studies focused on regional styles displaying well-defined paleographic features can prevent scholars from falling into elusive categories such as *sūdānī,* we will now concentrate on a description of the distinctive features of *barnāwī.*

[42] On this collection, see Mauro Nobili, "'Rediscovering' the de Gironcourt Manuscript Collection," *Annual Review of Islam in Africa* 1 (2008–2009): 62–66.

[43] Nobili, "Arabic Scripts in West African Manuscripts," 133.

[44] Brigaglia, "Central Sudanic Arabic Scripts (Part 1)," 80–83.

[45] See also two Qurʾanic manuscripts described in Manijfeh Bayani, Tim Stanley, and Anna Contadini, *The Nasser D. Khalili Collection of Islamic Art, Vol. IV, The Decorated Word: Qurans of the 17th to 19th Centuries AD, Part One* (New York: Nour Foundation, in association with Azimuth Editions and Oxford University Press, 1998), 35–39.

[46] The most ancient copy of the Qurʾan from Borno displays in margins different commentaries in Arabic, one of whom by al-Qurṭūbī (d. 671/1273) is dated 1st Jumādà II 1080/October 27, 1669 (Bivar, "A Dated Kuran from Bornu," 203). The latter date represents the *terminus ante quem* for the production of this copy.

Barnāwī: *A Brief Description*

Most of the distinctive features of *barnāwī* may be observed in the following pictures reproducing the *Sūra al-Fātiḥa* from five different Qurʾanic manuscripts from Borno (see figures 2–6). It must be noted that these features are common to all the manuscripts of the area, both Qurʾanic and non-Qurʾanic. As noted by Dmitry Bondarev, the difference between Qurʾanic and non-Qurʾanic hands that is often found elsewhere is not relevant in the case of Borno.[47] The same *barnāwī* script is employed in nineteenth-century diplomatic correspondence,[48] in the genealogical lists in Kanuri known as *Gargam,*[49] in Hausa *ʿajamī* poems,[50] and even in the hands of the interlinear glosses in Kanembu Qurʾanic exegesis peculiar to Borno, which one would expect to be written in a more ordinary and round (often referred to as "cursive") hand.[51] Thus, our decision to show different images of the same *sūra* of the Qurʾan is only to facilitate comparison and must not be taken as an indication that the script described here is reserved to the Qurʾan.

The overall appearance of *barnāwī* is bold and squat. The script tends to display the following features:

—the horizontal dimension of the script is emphasized to the detriment of the vertical one, and the graphemes vary little in height (for instance, a *qāf* or a *fāʾ* are generally as tall as the *kāf, lām,* or *alif*);
—the graphemes rest on a continuous, straight, horizontal baseline;
—the shape of the individual graphemes is straight and flat, with markedly angular junctions between the horizontal and vertical strokes;
—the spacing between the graphemes is regular and neat;
—the diacritic dots are often thick;
—the script is constantly serif-less.

[47] Dmitry Bondarev, "Multiglossia in West African Manuscripts: The Case of Borno, Nigeria," in *Manuscript Cultures: Mapping the Field,* ed. Jorg B. Quenzer, Jan U. Sobich, and Dmitry Bondarev (Berlin: De Gruyter, in press).
[48] Bivar, "Arabic Documents of Northern Nigeria."
[49] Bondarev, "Multiglossia in West African Manuscripts."
[50] See, for example, School of Oriental and African Studies (London), MS 380271: Hausa Islamic Poems collected by Capt. William B. G. Barne in 1906–1907.
[51] Bondarev, "Multiglossia in West African Manuscripts."

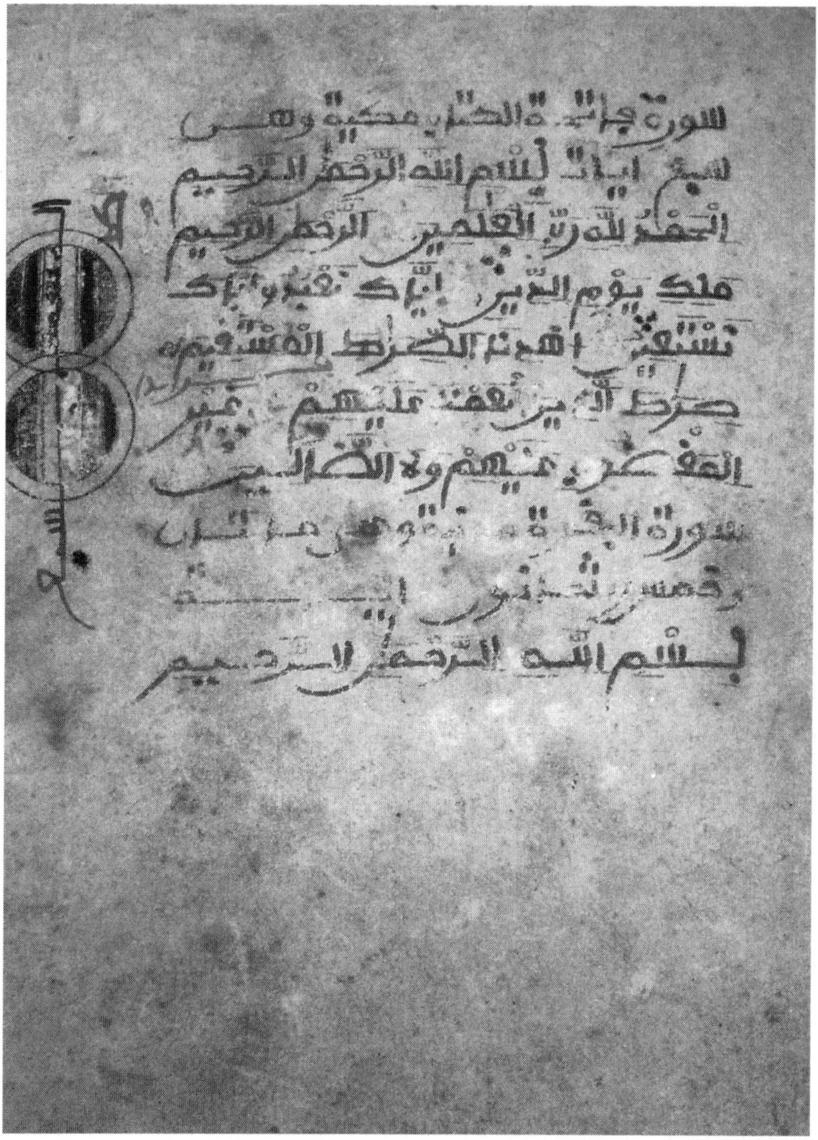

Figure 2. The *Sūra al-Fātiḥa* in a Bornuan manuscript (early twentieth century). Picture courtesy of Maimadu Barma Mutai (Ph.D. candidate, University of Maiduguri). Mutai has collected an impressive number of materials related to the Qurʾanic culture of Borno, and has kindly made several of these images available to the authors. The script displayed in these manuscripts is very consistent, allowing one to speak of a *barnāwī* script.

Figure 3. The *Sūra al-Fātiḥa* in a Bornuan manuscript (early twentieth century). Picture courtesy of Maimadu Barma Mutai. Borno has had a reputation for centuries in the disciplines of Qur'anic memorization and calligraphy. Students still travel to Borno from other areas of northern Nigeria, as well as from neighboring Niger Republic, Cameroon, Chad, and Central African Republic. The script used today in the Qur'anic schools of Borno is exactly the same as the script found on manuscripts (Qur'anic and non-Qur'anic) coming from the same area and dating back to the last 300 years.

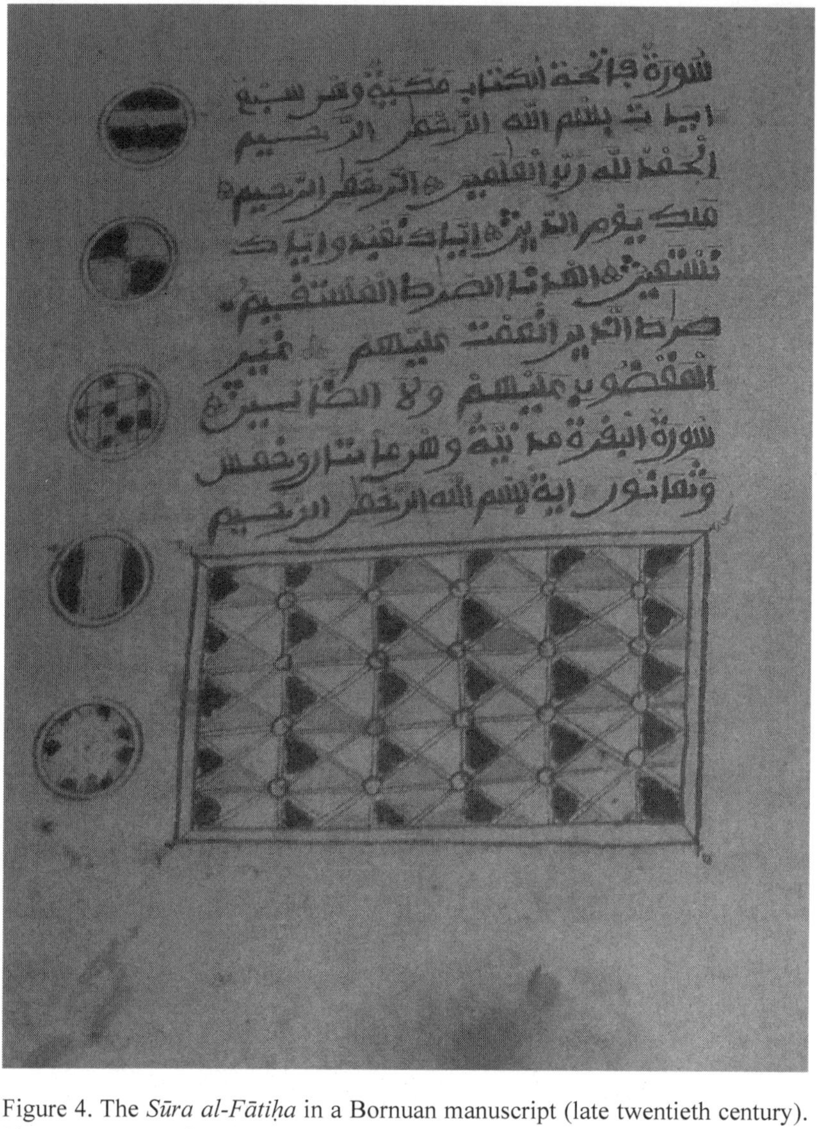

Figure 4. The *Sūra al-Fātiḥa* in a Bornuan manuscript (late twentieth century). Picture courtesy of Maimadu Barma Mutai. In traditional Qurʾanic schools, students study the Qurʾan by writing small portions on a wooden board, memorizing it, and washing it off before writing a new portion. The final stage of the process consists of writing a full copy of the Qurʾan on paper without mistakes. This method of study, which, though declining, is still practiced in the region, explains the ongoing production in Borno of a huge number of handwritten copies of the Qurʾan.

Figure 5. The *Sūra al-Fātiḥa* in a Bornuan manuscript (late twentieth century). Picture courtesy of Maimadu Barma Mutai. The angularity of the script, its continuous and straight baseline, the open *bāʾ*/*tāʾ*/*thāʾ* in their final position, the similar height of the letters (e.g., *qāf* and *fāʾ* are as tall as *alif* or *lām*), the presence of straight ascenders, and the flat *mīm* on the baseline joining at the bottom are all traits that suggest a direct link between the *barnāwī* script and early Arabic scripts like the *écriture livresque abbasside.* The roots of *barnāwī* exist in the period preceding the consolidation of *maghribī* in North Africa, around the eleventh or twelfth century.

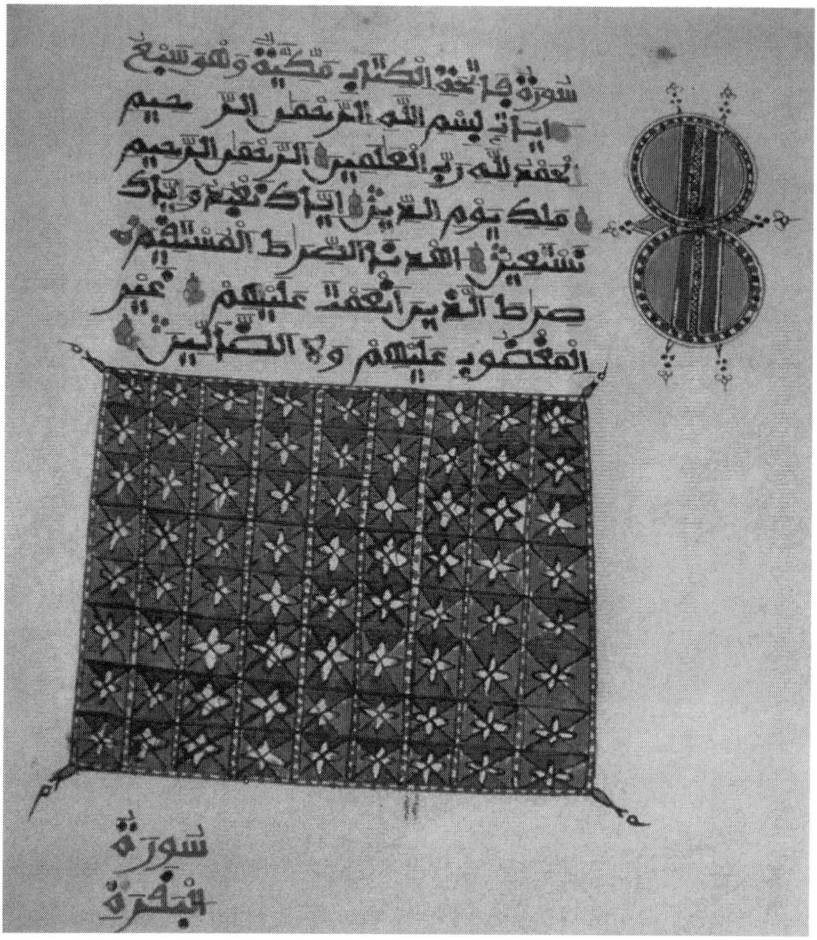

Figure 6. The *Sūra al-Fātiḥa* in a beautifully decorated manuscript in the handwriting of Gwani Kime (contemporary Yobe State, Nigeria). Picture courtesy of Maimadu Barma Mutai. The script of this manuscript is a traditional *barnāwī* enriched by serifs. Whereas most Bornuan manuscripts feature serifless scripts, it appears that the presence of serifs in this manuscript is a feature designed by the individual calligrapher to enhance the beauty of the script.

Figure 7. The *Sūra al-Fātiḥa* in a beautifully decorated manuscript in the typical handwriting of Kano. Picture courtesy of Andrea Brigaglia. The *kanawī* developed out of the *barnāwī* model and became popular around the middle of the twentieth century. Characterized by the thickness of the script, *kanawī* emphasizes the contrast between vertical or diagonal lines (drawn with the pointed tip of a reed pen) and the horizontal ones (drawn with the oblique edge).

When observing the presence of these features, one notices that *kanawī* is a peculiar realization of *barnāwī.* The former script, which is probably more recent, has maintained all the paleographic characteristics of the latter, developing it into a bolder, refined version. In cases like the one displayed here, *kanawī* (see figure 7) characteristically emphasizes the contrast between the vertical and diagonal lines—which are drawn with the pointed tip of the reed pen—and the horizontal ones—which are drawn with its oblique edge.

The general appearance of *barnāwī* and its offshoot (*kanawī*) clearly stands out against the round outlook of *ṣaḥrāwī.*[52] The latter, which is the typical script of the Sahelo-Saharan belt between Mauritania and western Mali, is characterized by a jagged baseline and the overlapping of certain graphemes. It is also important to note that both *barnāwī* and *ṣaḥrāwī* are script traditions of remarkably conservative attitudes. Just as *barnāwī* of the available manuscripts from the seventeenth century is one and the same with *barnāwī* used on the *lawḥ* (Qurʾanic slates) of today's Bornuan Qurʾanic schools, *ṣaḥrāwī* too shows an uninterrupted homogeneity through the centuries: the oldest known specimens of *ṣaḥrāwī,* which date back to the second half of the sixteenth century,[53] bear a striking resemblance to the script used in many manuscripts from twentieth-century Mauritania and northwestern Mali.[54]

The peculiarity of the Central Sudanic tradition can be better appreciated by looking at the same letters in *barnāwī* and in *ṣaḥrāwī.*

[52] For a discussion of *ṣaḥrāwī* with images, see Mauro Nobili, "Écriture et transmission du savoir islamique au Mali: Le cas du *ṣaḥrāwī,*" in *Dynamiques de transmission du savoir islamique au Mali,* ed. Elisa Pelizzeri and Omar Sylla (Paris: Harmattan, 2012), 35–68.

[53] See John O. Hunwick, "West African Arabic Manuscript Colophons," *Sudanic Africa* 12 (2002): 123–52.

[54] See, for an early twentieth-century manuscript from Timbuktu written in *ṣaḥrāwī,* Nobili, "Arabic Scripts in West African Manuscripts," 119.

Chart of letters comparing some paleographic features of *Barnāwī* and *Ṣaḥrāwī*

Barnāwī	*Ṣaḥrāwī*
The graphemes *bāʾ, tāʾ, thāʾ, nūn, yāʾ,* in initial and medial position, are realized as a straight denticle. 	This grapheme in initial and medial position is only a faint denticle. 
Bāʾ, tāʾ, thāʾ in final position are open to the left. 	In final position, this homograph is realized with a tail elongated toward the right, in the form of a comma turned upside down. 
The homograph *dāl/dhāl* usually sits on the baseline, with the downstroke below the baseline itself. At times, the two halves of the homograph are identical, forming a sort of horseshoe, equally divided by the baseline. 	The homograph does not develop much above the baseline, but consists mainly of a curved downstroke that develops under the baseline, resembling the homograph *rāʾ/zāʾ*. 
Rāʾ and *zāʾ* have the standard shape of a smooth descender developing to the left below the baseline. 	This homograph is in most cases hooked. When joined to the preceding letter, it may be written under it, forming a slope. 
The denticles of the *sīn* and the *shīn* are perpendicular to the baseline. They are tall and have the same height. They are usually written by lifting the pen for each denticle. 	The shape of this homograph resembles a saw, and it is realized with a single stroke. 
The ascender of the *ṭāʾ/ẓāʾ* is in most cases perpendicular to the baseline. The dot of the *ẓāʾ* is always written to the right of the descender. 	The ascender of this homograph is realized obliquely. The dot of the *ẓāʾ* is written to the left of the ascender. 
Initial and medial *fāʾ/qāf* are always raised on a stalk. Final *fāʾ* is also raised and left open to the left. Final *qāf,* on the contrary, is not raised, and the tail has the shape of a bowl. When completed, both graphemes are unpointed. 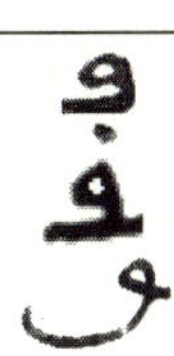	*Fāʾ* and *qāf* lay on the baseline in the form of a simple circle. The counter is in most cases closed, resembling a circular spot of ink. When final, the grapheme is unpointed. 

(*Continued on p. 216*)

Barnāwī	*Ṣaḥrāwī*
The *mīm* is a neat semicircle, with its bottom side flat on the baseline. In some cases, the grapheme has the shape of a smooth triangle. If connected, the *mīm* joins at the bottom, both to the previous letter and to the following one. When final, the tail is usually straight and perpendicular to the baseline, and the grapheme might tend toward the shape of a smooth triangle. 	The *mīm* is realized as a simple circle. The counter is often closed, resembling a circular spot of ink. When joined, it may be written under the preceding letter, forming a sort of slope. In its final position, the tail is undulating. 
The homograph *hā'/tā' marbūṭa* in isolated position is usually round. Sometimes it has the shape of a smooth triangle. 	This homograph in isolated position is realized in the shape of a big inverted comma standing on the baseline. 
In initial and medial position it is realized as a double semicircle or a double square, lying flat on the baseline. 	In its initial and medial position it might be realized in two different shapes: the first resembles a cypher "8" bending to the left and lying on the baseline; the second resembles the Latin letter "v" written below the baseline. 
In its final position, it has the shape of a simple semi-circle or smooth triangle on the baseline. 	In its final position, the homograph is usually realized as a simple downward stroke, right to left. 

The Origins of **Barnāwī**

Many scholars, as noted above, have pointed out the peculiarity of the style of Borno. The only genuine attempt to sketch a theory of the historical development of *barnāwī,* however, was made by Adrian D. H. Bivar. In a 1968 article, Bivar formulated for the first time the theory that this writing style, which he called "Bornu court hand," may not constitute a subtype of the *maghribī,* but could be considered a descendant of an earlier "Kufic script" through a now extinct Tunisian *ifrīqī.*[55]

[55] Adrian D. H. Bivar, "The Arabic Calligraphy of West Africa," *African Language Review* 7 (1968): 3–15 (and plates i–viii).

According to Bivar's hypothesis, the Borno court hand/*barnāwī* shows a distinctive boldness and an angularity that are reminiscent of the "Kufic": "Its distinctive feature is the angularity of the script, and its close conformity with the outlines of the Kufic character, noticeable is the thick, heavy line of the letters, and in particular the elongated form of the letter *kāf*."[56] Aware of the elusive nature of the term, Bivar cautiously pointed out that "Kufic is used here in its broad general sense, as covering all the angular forms of monumental Arabic script."[57] Western (*maghribī*) variants of the Kufic, continued Bivar, were used in the eleventh century by the Almoravids in Morocco and earlier by the Fatimids in Tunisia. In North Africa, this script was gradually replaced by thinner, more "cursive" styles popularized by the Andalusian calligraphers who started to migrate to North Africa after the successive waves of the Christian reconquest of al-Andalus. Based on a section of the *Muqaddima* in which Ibn Khaldūn describes the scripts used in North Africa in his time, Bivar highlights how, in the fourteenth century, the primitive Kufic script had survived only in the desert oases of southern Tunisia (Ifrīqiyā). It is this script (*ifrīqī*) and not any later version of the *maghribī* that according to Bivar must be identified as the link between the Borno hand and its "Kufic" ancestor: "The *older* traditions survived as we have seen in Bornu, and a near descendant of the original Ifrīqī was still in use as the court hand [of the Borno Empire]."[58]

This hypothesis has been taken on in different ways by Adrian Brockett and Salah Hassan.[59] In an article that analyzes a Qurʾan from northern Nigeria, Brockett provides a description of a hand that resembles "the older Kufi."[60] This script is called by Brockett indifferently (and confusingly) *"Sūdānī Maghribī,"*[61] "Ifrīqī,"[62] and "Bornu Ifrīqī hand."[63] Its resemblance to the older, monumental "Kufic," concludes Brockett,

[56] Ibid., 7.

[57] Bivar, "The Arabic Calligraphy," 15, n. 14.

[58] Ibid., 9 (emphasis added).

[59] Adrian Brockett, "Aspects of the Physical Transmission of the Qurʿān in 19th-century Sudan: Script, Decoration, Binding and Paper," *Manuscripts of the Middle East* 2 (1987): 45–67; Hassan, *Art and Islamic Literacy* (especially the chapter "Arabic Malamic Calligraphy: Genealogy and the Making of a Style," 116–47).

[60] Brockett, "Aspects of the Physical Transmission," 46.

[61] Ibid., 45.

[62] Ibid., 45–46.

[63] Ibid., 46.

supports the theory that it "is an *earlier* branch of the overall Maghribi tradition."[64]

In the chapter on calligraphy in his book about Qurʾanic arts among the Hausa of Kano, Hassan follows very closely the historical model that had been proposed by Bivar. Hassan points out that all the variants of Arabic script used in northern Nigeria can be traced back to a Bornuan model, which in turn "was derived from the *earlier* varieties of the *maghribi* script, and in particular the *Qairawani* style,"[65] by which he most likely means Bivar's *ifrīqī.*

The theory of the antiquity of the origins of the Borno hand and of its filiation from an *ifrīqī* model has been harshly criticized by Stanley.[66] According to the latter, a manuscript donated as *ḥubs* in Qayrawān in 406/1015, which shows some features of the eastern script tradition, discards the possibility that the Borno Qurʾanic manuscripts—which, on the contrary, display western features—are derived from the *ifrīqī* script apparently used in Qayrawān. Stanley also adds a historical critique to Bivar's argument: the Almoravids, whom Bivar—according to Stanley—considered responsible for introducing the *ifrīqī* script in West Africa, never controlled Tunisia, and their conquest of the ancient empire of Ghana is not accepted anymore as a historical fact.[67] The *ifrīqī,* concludes Stanley, "was not a member of the Maghribi group of scripts, whereas the Sudanese [*sic!*] hand is."[68] Echoing Stanley's argument, Blair states that "Bivar's arguments are ultimately unsatisfactory for a variety of reasons, ranging from historical to palaeographic."[69]

The authors of the present article believe that this critique is weak. Focusing on their criticism of the idea of the Almoravid origin of the Borno hands, Stanley and Blair seem to have lost sight of the essence of Bivar's main argument. For Bivar, the point was not so much proving an Almoravid origin—which, in fact, he only explicitly claims for the well-known inscriptions on the tombstones from Almeria found in Gao and first described by Sauvaget.[70] The essence of Bivar's argument was that it

[64] Ibid. (emphasis added).

[65] Hassan, *Art and Islamic Literacy,* 125 (emphasis added).

[66] Stanley, "The Qurʾanic Script of Western Sudan."

[67] Ibid., 34.

[68] Ibid.

[69] Blair, *Islamic Calligraphy,* 573.

[70] See Jean Sauvaget, "Les epitaphes royales de Gao," *Bulletin de l'Institut Fondamental d'Afrique Noire* 12 (1950): 418–40.

is possible to derive the Borno script "from the varieties of monumental Kufic scripts used in the Far West by the Almoravids during the Fifth century of the Hijra (i.e., AD 1009–1106) and by the Fāṭimids in Tunisia at a somewhat earlier date."[71] Therefore, Bivar argued, the Borno script tradition "does not itself derive from the . . . *fās* tradition [i.e., *maghribī*], and in fact represents a quite distinct and *much more archaic* style."[72] The model from which the Borno hand is supposed to have developed was not restricted by Bivar to the script of the Almoravids, but was identified in what we could call, rephrasing his argument, an earlier *substratum* shared by most North African hands before the emergence of the *maghribī* script.

The studies by François Déroche of the early scripts employed in Arabic manuscripts have demonstrated the existence of a common substratum of scripts called "écriture livresque Abbasside" and used in both the eastern regions of the Muslim world (*mashriq*) and the western ones (*maghrib*) until the tenth century CE.[73] Déroche underlines how the Maghreb at that time was not yet characterized by a peculiar script: "Even if the Maghreb interpreted the Oriental styles in its own way, especially with regards to the script, it did not differ substantially from them."[74] It was only in the second half of the tenth century, continues Déroche, that a new style started to emerge in North Africa out of the earlier *écriture livresque Abbasside;* this style, the *maghribī,* eventually established itself in the eleventh century as the peculiar script of the region.[75]

The unusual features of *maghribī* are described by Déroche in another contribution specifically devoted to this style.[76] One will notice that many of the features that Déroche says distinguish *maghribī* from the earlier scripts are usually absent in *barnāwī:* the ligatures of the letters breaking up the baseline and giving it the shape of a saw; final and isolated *bāʾ* (as well as *tāʾ* and *thāʾ*) with a pronounced tail that has the shape of an inverted comma; initial *ʿayn* (and *ghayn*) with exaggerated dimensions; *lām,* as well as the other stems, curved to the left; and connected *mīm* that does

[71] Bivar, "The Arabic Calligraphy," 7.

[72] Ibid., 7 (emphasis added).

[73] François Déroche, *Le livre manuscrit arabe: Préludes à une histoire* (Paris: Bibliothèque Nationale de France, 2004), 69.

[74] Ibid., 73.

[75] Ibid., 75.

[76] François Déroche, "O. Houdas et les écritures maghrébines," in *Le manuscrit arabe et la codicologie,* ed. Ahmed-Chouqui Binebine (Rabat: Université Mohammed V, 1994), 75–81.

not join at the bottom.[77] Such characteristic features of *maghribī* were later amplified when this script underwent another transformation with the diaspora of Spanish Muslims following the "Reconquista," which culminated in the 1492 fall of Granada. In the words of Sheila Blair, "calligraphers continued to use the same script found earlier in the region. . . . Repetition only led to exaggeration."[78]

The absence of these features suggests that the origins of *barnāwī* should be traced back to a period prior to the establishment of the *maghribī* script in North Africa. The angularity of the script, its continuous and straight baseline, the open *bāʾ/tāʾ/thāʾ* in their final position, the absence of exaggerated dimensions of the letters, the presence of straight ascenders, and the flat *mīm* on the baseline joining at the bottom are all traits that suggest the antiquity of the origins of the *barnāwī* script and its direct link to *écriture livresque abbasside.*

The absence of Borno manuscripts from the period prior to the seventeenth century prevents us from knowing the full outline of the development of the script of the region. The presence in *barnāwī* of features found in *écriture livresque Abbasside* but absent from *maghribī,* however, leads us to a hypothesis about the origins of the Borno hand that closely resembles Bivar's argument.

The obvious counterclaim to the assertion that *barnāwī* may not have been derived from *maghribī* is the presence of a peculiar, "western" diacritical pointing: *fāʾ* with one dot below the grapheme and *qāf* with one dot above it. This is the main paleographic proof Stanley employs to question Bivar's theory of the parallel and independent development of the Borno hands and the *maghribī.*[79] It should be stressed, however, that Déroche does not mention this particular trait in his list of the distinctive features of the *maghribī.* The presence of the "western" diacritical pointing of the *fāʾ* and the *qāf* has in fact been noted in manuscripts produced in different areas of the Muslim world—both "west" and "east"—that date back to the first/seventh century. This shows that the peculiar punctuation of *fāʾ* and *qāf,* which later became the "trademark" of the North African script tradition, was not originally restricted to the Maghreb.[80]

[77] Ibid., 79.

[78] Blair, "Islamic Calligraphy," 566.

[79] Stanley, "The Qurʾanic Script of Western Sudan," 34.

[80] François Déroche et al., *Islamic Codicology: An Introduction to the Study of Manuscripts in Arabic Script* (London: al-Furqan Islamic Heritage Foundation, 2005), 220–21.

Another possible (and stronger) objection could be the presence in *barnāwī* of the grapheme *ṣād/ḍād* devoid of denticle.[81] According to Déroche, this trait emerged with *maghribī* and remained one of its most distinctive features.[82] It is not possible to know exactly when *barnāwī* adopted this trait. The fact is not, in itself, surprising as the scribes of Borno were always exposed to writings of *maghribī* origin. For this reason, we have preferred to focus more on the traits that *distinguish barnāwī* from *maghribī* than the ones they have in common. If one accepts the theory that *barnāwī* derives from *maghribī,* one would have to justify the coincidence whereby the Borno scribes, in modifying certain characteristics of the *maghribī,* so closely reproduced the model of an earlier, extinct ancestor of the script they had supposedly acquired. It would be hard, for instance, to justify why, after adopting a script like *maghribī* in which the grapheme *bāʾ/tāʾ/thāʾ* in final position usually has a long tail in the shape of an inverted comma, the scribes of Borno decided to opt for an open-ended realization of the same grapheme, faithfully reproducing a trait of *écriture livresque abbasside* that had become exceptionally rare in the North African script tradition.

Conclusion

In light of the "discovery" of an increasing number of West African collections and of the availability of images of many manuscripts from the region, the assumption that West Africa is characterized by one Arabic script (*sūdānī*) is now unsustainable. Although it had passed unnoticed in most previous literature, ample evidence shows the existence of different regional scripts displaying a high degree of internal consistency. This paper has focused on the Central Sudanic script, analyzing the paleographic features of its oldest subtype, *barnāwī,* and discussing the latter's historical origins.

Barnāwī shows traits that are absent in the post-eleventh-century *maghribī* script. This article is not suggesting that *maghribī* had no influence at all in Saharan and sub-Saharan Africa; on the contrary, *maghribī* is certainly the source of West African scripts such as *ṣaḥrāwī,* as its paleographic description clearly demonstrates. Furthermore, preliminary research on manuscripts from parts of Mali, Senegal, and Gambia shows

---

[81] We are thankful to Dmitry Bondarev for correctly drawing our attention to this point.

[82] Déroche, "O. Houdas et les écritures maghrébines," 79.

that their script too displays some influence of the *maghribī*, namely in the presence of an isolated *hāʾ/tāʾ marbūṭa* in the shape of an inverted comma, and *ṭāʾ/ẓāʾ* with a slant ascender and dot written to its left.[83]

Contrary to *maghribī* features, *barnāwī* displays features that characterize what has been called by François Déroche *écriture livresque abbasside*. This style predates the emergence of *maghribī* in North Africa. On the same line Sheila Blair, in her meticulous description of the adoption and proliferation of round scripts, suggests that a more angular style—which she calls "broken cursive" and which corresponds to Déroche's *écriture livresque abbasside*—was substituted by *maghribī* in the eleventh century.[84] An analysis of the features presented by Blair as characteristic of the "broken cursive" confirms the proximity of *barnāwī* to this model.

The antiquity of the features that distinguish *barnāwī* from *maghribī* strengthens the hypothesis that the first cannot derive from the second. This argument, already advanced by Adrian D. H. Bivar and strongly criticized by Tim Stanley and Blair, points to the early second millennium as the period of first development of a distinctive script tradition in Borno, in a period that predates the emergence in North Africa of *maghribī* out of *écriture livresque abbasside*. It is impossible, however, to identify a specific moment in which *écriture livresque abbasside* was replaced by *maghribī*. The shift occurred gradually over a protracted span of time, possibly with continuous overlap between different styles and the coexistence of different scripts. Déroche had already noted that the emergence of *maghribī* "should not lead one to believe that the adoption of the new style was unanimous and simultaneous in the western part of the Islamic world."[85] In North Africa, Ifrīqiyā was particularly refractory to this change in script and still showed traces of the ancient style in the fifth/twelfth century.[86] However, since the *maghribī* script solidified in the early thirteenth century, it has maintained its distinctive traits until the modern era, as shown by Stanley in his presentation of the North African Qurʾanic manuscripts from the Khalili Collection.[87]

---

[83] Nobili, "Écriture et transmission du savoir," 59–62.

[84] See Blair, *Islamic Calligraphy*, 221–28.

[85] Déroche, "Houdas et les écritures maghrébines," 80.

[86] Ibid.

[87] See Tim Stanley, "North Africa: The Maintenance of a Tradition," in *The Nasser D. Khalili Collection of Islamic Art, Vol. IV, The Decorated Word: Qurʾans of the 17th to 19th Centuries AD, Part One*, ed. Manifjeh Bayani, Tim Stanley, and Anna Contadini (New York: Nour Foundation, in association with Azimuth Editions and Oxford University Press, 1998),

The claim of the distinctiveness of the Borno script must not be understood as an assertion of the cultural isolation of the region from the rest of the Muslim world. Just as the *maghribī* scribes who kept their distinctive style were certainly exposed to the eastern ones, any scholar from Borno since the spread of Islam in the area would have been exposed to various influences. Books were traveling to Central Sudan from Timbuktu and other centers of learning in sub-Saharan Africa, from Andalusia and the main centers of the Maghreb, from Egypt and the Fezzan, and from the Arabian Peninsula. The Muslim sovereigns of Borno corresponded with their North African and Ottoman counterparts. Borno was visited by Muslims from other parts of the Muslim world, while scholars and traders from Borno traveled beyond the borders of Central Africa. As a consequence, while *barnāwī* maintained its peculiarity through the centuries, it is perfectly possible that individual hands from the region might reveal traits that can be traced back to one or more outside influences.

To conclude, our article has suggested that the Central Sudanic family should not be seen as the offshoot of the *maghribī* tradition, but as its *cognate.* This was already suggested by Nico van den Boogert, who—in what is still the only contribution entirely devoted to the *maghribī* script in a western language after Houdas—purposely avoids including West Africa in his analysis. The script of this area, argued van den Boogert, "probably developed parallel to, but *independent from* the script of the Maghrib, and should be treated as a *cognate* to the Maghribi script as a whole."[88]

42–45. See also the handwritten copies of the Qurʾan from the Maghreb described in *The Nasser D. Khalili Collection of Islamic Art, Vol. IV,* 46–54.

[88] Nico van den Boogert, "Some Notes on Maghribi Script," *Manuscripts of the Middle East* 4 (1987): 31 (emphasis added). Boogert uses the term *sūdānī,* which we criticize; his observation, nonetheless, is particularly to the point for the Central Sudanic.

In Praise of the Intercessor: *Mawāhib al-Nāfiᶜ fī Madāʾiḥ al-Shāfiᶜ* by Amadu Bamba Mbacké (1853–1927)

Translated by Rudolph Ware, UNIVERSITY OF MICHIGAN

DOI: 10.5192/215409930402225

ABSTRACT

In Praise of the Intercessor is an effort to capture in English verse an echo of the original meaning, rhythm, and tenor of a panegyric written by one of West Africa's most famous Sufi shaykhs, Amadu Bamba. The founder of the Muridiyya wrote literally hundreds of distinct works in Arabic verse, but the piece translated here is one of his most widely recited poems, and the translation notes here expound upon the significance of some his poetic allusions for Murids. The introduction offers reflections on the role of praise poetry in Islamic scholarly culture, as well as the challenges and immense rewards in translating such works in fresh ways.

Foreword

The following piece is part of a larger project, directed by the Institute for the Study of Islamic Thought in Africa (ISITA) and generously supported by the Ford Foundation. The goal of this single part of ISITA's many research programs is to produce an English-language anthology of the writings of three famous Senegambian Sufi scholars: Al-Ḥājj ᶜUmar Taal (d. 1864), Amadu Bamba Mbacké (d. 1927), and Shaykh Ibrāhīm

Islamic Africa, VOL. 4, NO. 2, 2013. ISSN 2154-0993.

Niass (d. 1975). In this and forthcoming issues of this journal, we will present translations of some of the works connected with the production of that anthology.

These three individuals, all of whom were born within roughly one hundred years and two hundred miles of one another in families that specialized in religious scholarship, came to be among the most widely read *African* intellectuals of the nineteenth and twentieth centuries in any language. Each was also among the most prodigious writers of his respective time. *Arabic Literature of Africa: Volume* 4, *Writings of Western Sudanic Africa* records no less than 310 distinct entries for the three men taken together, and this certainly *underestimates* their productivity. They represented, for greater Senegambia, the efflorescence of the classical tradition of Islamic *scholarship,* meaning here closely related phenomena of *schooling* and *scholarly* production.

By schooling we mean to evoke traditional training in the religious sciences (*al-ʿulum al-dīniyya*), and we explicitly include *taṣawwuf,* the science of spiritual purity, among those disciplines. Each of the three authors above was considered by many of his contemporaries to be the greatest living Sufi saint of his time, the pole of the era (*quṭb al-zamān*). None had such claims accepted without some contestation, but such high praise came not only from their respective disciples, but also from other Muslims, who saw them as embodiments of sanctity and piety. During their lifetimes, they were magnetic spiritual authorities. Muslims of all backgrounds flocked to their Sufi paths—sometimes leaving other ways—to follow in their footsteps.

Because of their mass appeal, Taal, Mbacké, and Niass were all closely watched by the political authorities of their lifetimes, which spanned the precolonial, colonial, and postcolonial periods of West African history. The French colonial state began its mainland conquests during the height of Al-Ḥājj ʿUmar's career as a saint and state-builder, forcing him to abandon his goals of expanding his polity into his homeland of Fuuta Tooro. The French arbitrarily arrested, imprisoned, and exiled Bamba to Gabon for seven years from 1895 to 1902 and forced him to live under house arrest until the end of his life. Both British and French colonial governments spied on the activities of Shaykh Ibrāhīm throughout his lifetime. According to internal narratives, all three men were also targets of planned assassination attempts by European authorities.

These were men who drew the attention of their contemporaries, for better and for worse. Their respective personalities, leadership qualities, and institutional frameworks were distinctive, but all were intimately tied to their Arabic writings. Each man drew on his corpus of writings as tangible proof of saintly and scholarly pedigree, and it is time for Africanists and Islamicists to pay much closer attention to their words.

The larger anthology will attempt to open up their writings, not simply by rendering them in English, but also by contextualizing them within the life trajectories and spiritual travels of their authors. We have selected three pieces of writing from each master, from three distinct phases of their lives and evolutions as Sufis. It is significant, however, that after reaching intellectual and spiritual maturity, and composing didactic and expository works in the religious science, all three men focused nearly all of their later literary production on *madḥa* (panegyric praise poetry). Here, in the pages of *Islamic Africa,* in our serialized engagement with these authors, we have chosen to present excerpts from this last genre and spiritual station. These are, unquestionably, the most difficult works to translate. Perhaps more than other genres of writing, *madḥa* are designed to produce a moral and emotional state within the hearer. They do this through extraordinary use of the Arabic language, rich imagery, and powerful rhythm. It is here that the great shaykhs were also often the most experimental and original in deploying their own unique literary styles.

Now, long after their passing, disciples of all three men are spread throughout West Africa and the world. It is no exaggeration to say that the Sufi disciples of the writers of these works number today in the tens of millions. They are loved as saints and respected as scholars by many millions more. There are massive efforts underway by members of the Tijāniyya and Murīdiyya Sufi movements to acquaint new audiences with the timeless message of these scholars. In the sources section of this important journal, *Islamic Africa,* we hope to make a humble scholarly contribution to this noble effort.

Rudolph Ware, Amir Syed, and Zachary Wright

In Praise of the Intercessor: Mawāhib al-Nāfiᶜ fī Madāʾiḥ al-Shāfiᶜ

If a picture is worth a thousand words, how many words for He who cannot be pictured? The Islamic tradition forbids visual representation of its most beloved and respected exemplar of piety, the Prophet Muhammad. Thus, all the beauty and devotion that one finds in other religious traditions expressed in visual or plastic arts is predominantly rendered in verse within the Islamic tradition. Visualize for a moment all that was *communicated* in Egyptian religious statuary, the lost Buddhas of Bamiyan, Michelangelo's Pietà or the Sistine Chapel. This gives a partial sense of what prayers, praise, and poetry dedicated to the Prophet have communicated for many Muslims. *Madḥa,* panegyric praise poetry (especially to honor the Prophet), is, in a manner of speaking, the *monument* of the Islamic tradition. It is the artistic edifice raised to honor the man who bore the Qurʾan and who, in Islamic eschatology, will intercede with God on behalf of his community. But all of this poses special challenges of translation, for how would one *translate* the Sistine Chapel?

The beginnings of an answer, I think, are to be found in the approach to translation suggested here by Walter Benjamin: "The task of the translator . . . may be regarded as distinct and clearly differentiated from the task of the poet . . . [it] consists in finding that intended effect (intention) upon the language into which he is translating which produces in it the *echo* of the original."[1] I began this project in utter ignorance of Benjamin's essay.[2] Yet, I had a long-standing concern that the few efforts to translate the poems of the great African scholars of Islam into English often produced technically competent translations, but not necessarily poetic works.

There are, of course, exceptions to this rule. Souleymane Bachir Diagne's translation of Abbas Sall's poetry—to take but one example—captures the *rhythm* of Wolof verse beautifully, though it does not rhyme in English. There is a particular sensory effect that is produced by *rhyme,* whether in Arabic, Wolof, English, or any other language; my argument in translating this particular poem is that the *echo* simply cannot be reproduced without rhyme. Note the role of rhyming in the statement by Wolof poet Moussa Ka—cited in Diagne's essay—who was encouraged by Bamba to reduce to writing the Wolof praise poems he had already authored and to compose new verses: "Let me tell this to those who say that

[1] Walter Benjamin, *Illuminations* (Boston: Houghton Mifflin Harcourt, 1968), 76

[2] Thanks to my colleague at Michigan, Ellen Poteet, for bringing it to my attention.

writing in Wolof is not appropriate: rhyming in Wolof or in the noble Arabic language or in any other is the same. Any language you use to praise the Prophet of God will then reveal its innermost value."[3]

Rhyme, of course, is not *sufficient* to make a poem, but in the Arabic scholarly tradition one can argue that it is *necessary.* Much more than this is needed, however, for many pieces rendered in verse—including many of Bamba's own works—are perhaps best described as rhymed prose.[4] It is worth recalling that in nineteenth- and early twentieth-century Africa, Muslim writers used verse for most sorts of public writing. The novel as a genre was hardly known, and even analytical essays and commentaries in the religious sciences were often rendered in verse. So too were letters and other forms of writing. In nearly all of Bamba's expository writing, he employs rhyme.[5] But there seem to be significant distinctions in the purposes of rhyme in different sorts of writing. In the preamble to *Masālik al-Jinān,* Bamba specifically states that he has rendered the work in verse so that it can be more easily memorized.[6] It is precisely the *intention* of the rhyme in *madḥa* that separates it from more explicitly didactic works like *Masālik al-Jinān* or *Nahj Qād al-Hāj,* which are in verse but can still be meaningfully and powerfully translated in unrhymed prose.[7]

But in *madḥa* praise poetry, the memorable nature of the rhyme is, I believe, a secondary intention; the first is an attempt to produce a moral,

---

[3] Souleymane Bachir Diagne, "In Praise of the Tijaniyya," in *Tales of God's Friends: Islamic Hagiography in Translation,* ed. John Renard (Berkeley: University of California Press, 2009), 171.

[4] For European-language introductions to Bamba and his life, see Cheikh Anta Mbacké Babou, *Fighting the Greater Jihad: Amadu Bamba and the Founding of the Murīdiyya of Senegal, 1853–1913* (Athens: Ohio University Press, 2007); and Serigne Bachir Mbacké, *Les bienfaits de l'eternel: Ou la biographie de Cheikh Amadou Bamba Mbacké,* trans. Kadim Mbacké (Dakar: Institut Fondamental d'Afrique Noire, 1995).

[5] For a fine analysis and translation of a book of poetic meter composed by the man who taught Bamba this discipline during the latter's youth in the 1860s and 1870s, see Claudine Gerresch, "Le livre de métrique *Mubayyin al-ishkāl* du Cadi Madiakhaté Kala," *Bulletin de l'Institut Fondamental d'Afrique Noire* 36 (1974): 714–832.

[6] Amadu Bamba Mbacké, *Masālik al-Jinān,* ed. and trans. Sam Mbaye (Casablanca: Dar el Kitab, 1989).

[7] For the *Nahju*—a piece on the etiquette of pursuing religious knowledge—as well as other medium-length works in the traditional religious sciences with original Arabic and French translations, see Amadu Bamba Mbacké, *Diwān fī ʿulūm al-dīnīyya,* ed. and trans. Sam Mbaye (Casablanca: Dar el Kitab, 1989). Excerpts of both of these works are under translation for the proposed ISITA anthology of Senegambian Sufi writings.

emotional, and—I would insist—physical effect upon the hearer. These rhymes are meant, in part, to bypass the veil of reason altogether and enter the body directly. Thus, it is important that there be *hearers* rather than merely *readers.* The oral, aural, sensory, and emotive aspects of this kind of recitation are central to the purpose. I had a copy of this particular poem in my possession for a number of years, and I have occasionally thumbed through the pages reading the Arabic original or the accompanying French translation.[8] Neither of these sparked a sufficient interest in me to undertake such an effort. Rather, it was the *hearing* of this poem in a recitation by Serigne Abdoulaye Seck that made me absolutely determined to translate it.[9] I grasped perhaps a third of the words in the poem as I listened to its recitation in an absent-minded way. In no sense could I argue that the meaning of the poem produced any effect at all; instead, it was the rhythm and rhyme that affected me.

I had never read the poem aloud. I am now convinced that silent reading of Arabic poetry of this sort is a violation of one of its basic conditions of intelligibility. This focus on the auditory faculty befits a genre meant to be a poetic monument to the Prophet Muhammad, who sought to avoid idols and who could not read books, but who *listened* and *recited.* Such an exercise allows one to counter the tyranny of the visual in modern culture and see the image of the Prophet with the mind's eye or, one might say, with the eye of the heart.

Another basic element of the intention of the poem is that the writing—or rather, the composing—of it was clearly a devotional exercise. This became clear to me only after having spent several weeks straining to voice a faint English echo of the Arabic original. Finally, these are exercises at stretching the bounds of the language through virtuoso performance. Upon his return from exile in Gabon, Amadu Bamba maintained that among the many divine gifts (*mawāhib*) he had been given while he was there was a linguistic facility in Arabic that had never been attained by any non-Arab.

Benjamin argued that a crucial first step toward an effective translation was reflection on the *intention* of the original and a self-conscious assessment of whether it is even possible to create its *echo* in a language other

---

[8] Amadu Bamba Mbacké, *Diwān fī amdāḥ khayr al-mursalīn,* ed. and trans. Sam Mbaye (Casablanca: Dar el Kitab, 1989).

[9] http://www.youtube.com/watch?v=LqyMMVMwzZo&list=PLAE22D9A3A9520AF7&index=37.

than the original: "Translation is a mode. To comprehend it as mode one must go back to the original, for that contains the law governing the translation: its translatability. The question of whether a work is translatable has a dual meaning. Either: Will an adequate translator ever be found among the totality of its readers? Or, more pertinently: Does its nature lend itself to translation?"[10]

Are Bamba's works *translatable* by Benjamin's criteria? I maintain that this one, at least, is. Others challenge the limits of translatability in extreme ways. Bamba's acrostic poems, for example, might be particularly challenging to render effectively in a language other than Arabic, since they are built on using the letters of the Arabic alphabet to craft particular verses and achieve certain alliterative effects. Like poems written by many Islamic scholars, some are composed of letter combinations that have numerological as well as discursive values. Can one reproduce the hidden intentions of a poem that is written in reference to a concealed numerological code in another alphabet? *Mawāhib al-Nāfiʿ* has some of this in its form, but not necessarily in its content. It is composed of 166 verses, which corresponds to the numerological value of "*la ilaha illa Allah,*" the first part of the Muslim testimony of faith, "there is no god but God."

I am less optimistic in my reply to the first part of Benjamin's query, for obviously there can be no truly adequate translator of any great poet, and Bamba is certainly a great poet. The *Arabic Literature of Africa* series records over 200 separate works of poetry and prose by Bamba, and this certainly *underestimates* his productivity. Even outside of the Murīdiyya, in other Sufi traditions and in far-ranging geographic contexts from Nouakchott to Nigeria, Bamba has long been admired as an excellent and inspiring poet. Adequate translation of his work is a *very high standard.* Within the Murīdiyya, his writings are the proof of his sainthood in the same way that the Qurʾan was the proof of Muhammad's Prophethood. If the Qurʾan was Muhammad's major miracle, then Bamba's "seven tons" of writings were his own.

I certainly cannot claim to be an adequate translator of Bamba's poetry, but I have earnestly attempted to produce the *echo* of *Mawāhib al-Nāfiʿ.* Taking the insights from Moussa Ka and Walter Benjamin together, I have tried to mine the literary resources of the receiving language, English, to produce some version of the *echo, intention,* and *rhyme* of the Arabic original. In order to reproduce the intentionality of this sort of poetry, I made

[10] Benjamin, *Illuminations,* 70.

it a daily devotional exercise, attempting to translate four verses each day, regardless of other commitments, and I completed it in forty days.

I also resolved to try to render the poem in a style of verse that echoed the original. For this, I instituted a basic set of rules. First, each line of the original is composed of exactly twenty syllables. Each line of translation here reproduces this basic rhythm, though occasionally I have had to accept a verse of nineteen or twenty-one syllables in order to better express the meaning. I have long found efforts to translate every shade of meaning in an Arabic text unwieldy, since often the resultant European-language translation is two or three times as long as the Arabic original. While there are sound arguments for translating in this way, especially in didactic or expository texts, the results are rarely poetic.

At the same time, however, it was impossible to reproduce the exact rhyme scheme of the original poem without doing real violence to the meaning of the poem. Instead, I drafted the poem freely at first while listening to recitations of it in Arabic. I found that after translating a handful of verses, I had—quite unconsciously—developed a rhyme scheme that mirrored the original without precisely reproducing it. The meaning in the poem tended to travel in couplets, and my earliest translation drafts tended to group verses in pairs. Each line of the original Arabic poem ends with a *ḥamza,* a glottal stop, followed for grammatical and morphological reasons by either a short or a long vowel "i." English, because of an abundance of words that end with the vowel "y" or other long "e" sound, is unusually well-suited to capture this aspect of the sound of this particular piece of poetry. The broader genre of *qaṣīda* to which most *madḥa* belongs is usually marked by an invariable rhyme scheme on the final syllable of each verse. Yet I found that ending each verse in this way produced an unpleasant and somehow unrelenting rhyme in English, which also restricted my ability to capture the discursive meanings of the Arabic original. In the end, I elected to have every other couplet reproduce this long "e" sound in its final rhyme. Wherever possible, I have chosen vocabulary that enhances the alliteration and rhyme of the poem, while trying to capture the meaning of the original as closely as possible.

Benjamin's notes on translation suggest that, while rendering some version of the original meaning is important, mere *correlation* is not what translation is really about: "As regards the meaning, the language of a translation can—in fact, must—let itself go, so that it gives voice to the *intentio* of the original not as reproduction but as harmony, as a supplement to the language in which it expresses itself, as its own kind of *intentio*."[11] Approximating the *meaning* of a text in the receiving language is not the hallmark of good translation in Benjamin's terms, but rather producing something that is harmoniously tied to the original. He offers a final opening onto the kind of work under translation here:

> It should be pointed out that certain correlative concepts retain their meaning . . . if they are referred exclusively to man. One might, for example, speak of an unforgettable life or moment even if all men had forgotten it. If the nature of such a life or moment required that it be unforgotten, that predicate would not imply a falsehood but merely a claim not fulfilled by men, and probably also a reference to a realm in which it is fulfilled: *God's remembrance.*[12]

Benjamin is making an analogy about translation. He seems to mean that God would remember an unforgettable life even if all mankind forgot it and, analogously, even a text that never finds an adequate human translator is *translatable* in this sense. Here, I want to point to *God's Remembrance* (*dhikrullāhi*) in a somewhat different sense than the one intended by Benjamin. When Bamba returned from his exile to Gabon in 1902, he famously told his disciples to throw all of his previous writings into the sea. He did not mean this literally; rather, he was making a point. For the last twenty-five years of his life, Bamba wrote *madḥa* almost exclusively. With his writing practice, Bamba seemed to be saying that the *remembrance of God and His Prophet* was the noblest and best use of language. Perhaps this humble and inadequate translation of a single work by Bamba will inspire others to *echo* the words of the talented African Muslim poets. If Moussa Ka is right, then even the English language will discover something of its innermost value in praise of the Intercessor.

صلى الله عليه وسلم

[11] Ibid., 79.

[12] Ibid., 70.

Mawāhib al-Nāfiʿ fī Madāʾiḥ al-Shāfiʿ

Gifts of the Benefactor in Praise of the Intercessor

by Amadu Bamba Mbacké (1853–1927)

translation by Rudolph Ware

In the name of God, the Compassionate, the Merciful.
My Dear Lord and Most Gracious God! Blessings on our lord
Muhammad the opener of what was closed,
The seal of what came before, the champion of Truth by
Truth and the guide to Your Straight Path
And upon His family in due measure with His eminent status.[13]

And make this poem a way to Faith, Submission, Perfection, and Eternal Happiness.[14]
And may it gladden the Messenger of God—Blessings of God
Most High upon Him, along with Peace—
Wherever one might recite it, write it, or gaze upon it, forevermore. Amen! O Lord of the Worlds!

And make it among those sung by the wide-eyed houris and
youths in the Paradise promised to the pious.
And make it among those loved and appreciated by You
and by Him—upon Him Prayers and Peace![15]

1. *By the name of God, bliss grows within me, free of limitation, without limit.*
2. *Praise the Lord and Master! He swelled my heart, through imitation of His Prophet.*

3. *For Him all my thanks without infidelity. He is my Aid. He set me free.*[16]
4. *No exile from Him in my intimacy, and so I speak to Him directly:*

5. *You're my contentment, of You I praise all. I count on You, and upon You I call.*
6. *You who healed me, You who shield me, from what malady or tyranny might befall.*[17]

7. *Drape me with Your veils of honor. Set right my deeds. Increase my blessings endlessly.*[18]
8. *You who answer whosoever may call, please answer my appeal and hear this plea!*

9. *Lord of Beauty, Lord of Majesty, refine my happiness, You're the best of friends.*[19]
10. *Lord of Oneness, Lord of Existence. Be generous with me, without any end.*

شَيْخُنَا لُوحْ نغَابُ

بِلاَلْ عَبْدُ الْحَقِّ رَدُلْفَ وَارْ

بِسْمِ اللهِ الرَّحْمَنِ الرَّحِيمِ

وَصَلَّى اللهُ عَلَى سَيِّدِنَا مُحَمَّدٍ وَ عَلَى آلِهِ وَصَحْبِهِ وَسَلَّمَ تَسْلِيمًا

مَوَاهِبُ النَّافِعِ فِي مَدَائِحِ الشَّافِعِ

بِسْمِ اللهِ الرَّحْمَانِ الرَّحِيمِ اللَّهُمَّ يَا أَكْرَمُ صَلِّ عَلَى سَيِّدِنَا مُحَمَّدٍ الْفَاتِحِ لِمَا أُغْلِقَ وَالْخَاتِمِ لِمَا سَبَقَ نَاصِرِ الْحَقِّ بِالْحَقِّ وَالْهَادِي إِلَى صِرَاطِكَ الْمُسْتَقِيمِ وَعَلَى آلِهِ حَقَّ قَدْرِهِ وَمِقْدَارِهِ الْعَظِيمِ وَاجْعَلْ هَذِهِ الْأَمْدَاحَ جَالِبَةً إِلَى الْإِيمَانِ وَالْإِسْلَامِ وَالْإِحْسَانِ وَإِلَى السَّعَادَةِ الدَّائِمَةِ وَفَرِّحْ بِهَا رَسُولَ اللهِ صَلَّى اللهُ عَلَيْهِ وَسَلَّمَ حَيْثُ قُرِأَتْ أَوْ كُتِبَتْ أَوْ نُظِرَ إِلَيْهَا أَبَدًا آمِينْ يَا رَبَّ الْعَالَمِينَ وَاجْعَلْهَا مِمَّا تَتَغَنَّى بِهَا الْحُورُ الْعِينُ وَالْوِلْدَانُ فِي الْجَنَّةِ الَّتِي وُعِدَ الْمُتَّقُونَ وَاجْعَلْهَا مِنْ أَحَبِّ الشُّكْرِ إِلَيْكَ وَإِلَيْهِ عَلَيْهِ الصَّلَاةُ وَالسَّلَامُ

1. بِسْمِ الْإِلَهِ يَنمُو لُهَائِي بِلاَ مَنَاهِ وَلاَ انْتِهَاءِ
2. حَمْدًا لِرَبٍّ خَيْرَ مُرَبٍّ قَدْ رَمَّ قَلْبِي بِالْإِقْتِدَاءِ

3. لَهُ شُكُورِي بِلاَ كُفُورِ وَهْوَ نَصِيرِي مِنْهُ فِدَاءِ
4. لَهُ اقْتِرَابِي بِلاَ اغْتِرَابِ لَهُ خِطَابِي مَعَ اهْتِدَاءِ

5. لَكَ رِضَائِي لَكَ ثَنَائِي لَكَ الْتِجَائِي مَعَ اجْتِدَاءِ
6. يَا مَن شَفَانِي يَا مَنْ حَمَانِي عَمَّنْ جَفَانِي بِمَحْوِ دَاءِ

7. أَسْبِلْ سُتُورِي أَصْلِحْ أُمُورِي كَثِّرْ خُيُورِي بِلَا كِدَاءِ
8. يَا مَنْ أَجَابَا مَنِ اسْتَجَابَا هَبْ لِي إِجَابَا فِي ذَا النِّدَاءِ

9. يَا ذَا الْجَمَالِ يَا ذَا الْجَلَالِ يَا خَيْرَ وَالِ صَفِّ لُهَاءِ
10. يَا ذَا الْوُجُودِ يَا ذَا الْوُجُودِ كُنْ لِي بِجُودِ بِلَا انْتِهَاءِ

11. *Straighten my homecoming, free me of shortcoming, shroud me in mantles of beauty.*
12. *Strengthen my reading with understanding. Sweeten my worship with states of rhapsody.*

13. *You raised my station without migration. Through me guide my family clear of laments.*[20]
14. *Accept my penance; safeguard my surroundings, my Return, and my intelligence.*

15. *Rescue me from illusion and self-delusion; grant me support and victory.*
16. *You who are Exalted above all partners, bestow Your favor and perfect me!*

17. *Your gifts brought me rectitude, for them my gratitude, free of recrimination.*
18. *You're the Provider, and You've sufficed me. I honor You without exaggeration.*

19. *For You my thanks in my abodes. Yours is the Palace to dwell in eternally.*
20. *You who clothed me, You who quenched me, You who sheltered me from despondency*

21. *You are my goal, You are my pillar, irradiating my heart, the Light is Yours.*
22. *You tore away my faults, took away my doubts, and cleansed my chest, as with the Pure.*

23. *You fulfilled my journey, blessed my provisions, be good to me, as with the Godly.*
24. *Best of restorers! Care for me. As with the Sages, increase my capacities.*

25. *Grant me uprightness, not blameworthiness. Grant me charisma, by the Flag's Bearer*[21]
26. *By the Lovely, the Faultless and Lofty, By the Remedy who cures of error.*

27. *By the Servant, By the Beneficial, from whence flow miracles to the Saintly.*
28. *By the Favored, a lion in combat, fighting the damned, slaying the enemy.*

29. *By He whose cohort answered the call, dispelling distress with illumination.*
30. *By He of the battles, dispelling dismay, skeptics, cynics, and ostentation.*

31. *He is the Lucid. He is the Herald, bearing Good News. This is His elegy.*
32. *So I address Him, devoid of obstruction, accusation, or obstinacy:*

33. *O Best of creations! Yours are the gains. Yours are the gifts. Hallow these walls.*
34. *You're my elation, with no illusions. Refine my devotions. Brighten these halls.*

35. *Of you I'm speaking, without deviation. On you I'm leaning, continuously.*
36. *On the Day of Reward, may our guiding Lord, repay you all you give to me.*

37. *May my Lord reward You, You the most loving, and most beloved, without deprival.*
38. *I'm Your Servant. Wherever I stand, I won't abandon my quest for requital.*

39. *You're my protection, from the Deceiver, and from deception, which lead to misery.*
40. *You raised my rank. You assured me. By the Everlasting, grant this era to me!*[22]

41. *You erase tarnish, leaving clarity; to the King, You're my path of arrival.*[23]
42. *You are the Beautiful. I'm drawn to You. You are the Messenger without rival.*

11. صَفِّ وُصُولِي بِلَا غُفُولِ لِي جُدْ بِسُولِ جَمِّلْ رِدَاءِ
12. هَبْ لِي التِّلَاوَةْ مَعَ الْحَلَاوَةْ هَبْ لِي الدِّرَايَةْ لَدَى الْأَدَاءِ

13. أَصْلَحْتَ حَالِي بِلَا ارْتِحَالِي بِي اهْدِ عِيَالِي بِلَا بُكَاءِ
14. لِي اقْبَلْ مَتَابِي وَاحْمِ جَنَابِي وَصُنْ مَئَابِي جَوِّدْ ذَ كَائِي

15. قِنِي الْغَرُورَا وَامْحُ الْغُرُورَا هَبْ لِي نُصُورَا مَعَ اتِّكَاءِ
16. قُدْ لِي نَوَالَا يُنمِي كَمَالَا يَا مَنْ تَعَالَى عَن شُرَكَاءِ

17. زِدتَّ هُدَايَا قُدتَّ هَدَايَا لِي بِرِضَايَا دُونَ اشْتِكَاءِ
18. يَا خَيْرَ مُغْنِ أَغْنَى بِمَنٍّ عَلَيْهِ أُثْنِي بِلَا غَلَاءِ

19. لَكَ شُكُورِي عِنْدَ دُيُورِي يَا ذَا الْقُصُورِ بِلَا جَلَاءِ
20. يَا مَنْ كَسَانِي يَا مَن سَقَانِي يَا مَنْ حَمَانِي عَنِ الْخَلَاءِ

21. أَنْتَ مُرَادِي أَنْتَ عِمَادِي نَوِّرْ فُؤَادِي يَا ذَا الضِّيَاءِ
22. زَحْزَحْتَ عَيْبِي أَذْهَبْتَ رَيْبِي طَهَّرْتَ جَيْبِي كَا الْأَصْفِيَاءِ

23. أَنْهَيْتَ سَيْرِي طَيَّبْتَ مَيْرِي كُنْ لِّي بِخَيْرِ كَا الْأَتْقِيَاءِ
24. يَا خَيْرَ مُحْيِ كُنْ لِّي بِرَعْيِ وَ خَيْرِ سَعْيِ كَا الْأَذْكِيَاءِ

25. هَبْ لِي اسْتِقَامَةْ قِنِي الْمَلَامَةْ هَبْ لِي الْكَرَامَةْ بِذِي اللِّوَاءِ
26. بِذِي ٱلْجَمَالِ بِذِي ٱلْكَمَالِ بِذِي ٱلْمَعَالِ بِذِي الدَّوَاءِ

27. بِذِي ٱلْعِبَادَةْ بِذِي ٱلْإِفَادَةْ بِخَرْقِ عَادَةْ لِلْأَوْلِيَاءِ
28. بِذِي النَّوَالِ لَيْثِ ٱلْقِتَالِ مُرْدِي الرِّجَالِ الْأَشْقِيَاءِ

29. بِذِي الصَّحَابَةْ ذَوِي ٱلْإِجَابَةْ جَالِي الْكَئَابَةْ ذَوِي الضِّيَاءِ
30. بِذِي الْحُرُوبِ جَالِي الْكُرُوبِ نُورِ الْأَرِيبِ مَاحِي الرِّيَاءِ

31. ذَاكَ ٱلْمُنِيرُ ذَاكَ الْبَشِيرُ لَهُ أُشِيرُ بِذَا الثَّنَاءِ
32. لَهُ خِطَابِي بِلَا عِتَابِ وَلَا حِجَابِ وَ لَا عَنَاءِ

33. خَيْرَ الْبَرَايَا يَا ذَا ٱلْمَزَايَا يَاذَا الْعَطَايَا صَفِّ بِنَائِي
34. أَنْتَ سُرُورِي بِلَا غُرُورِ صَفِّ بُرُورِي نَوِّرْ فِنَائِي

35. فِيكَ أَقُولُ وَلَا أَعُولُ فِيكَ أَعُولُ بِلَا فَنَاءِ
36. عَنِّي جَزَاكَا رَبٌّ هَدَاكَا فَوْقَ مُنَاكَا يَوْمَ الْجَزَاءِ

37. جَزَاكَ رَبِّي يَا خَيْرَ حِبِّي خَيْرَ مُحِبٍّ بِلَا ارْتِزَاءِ
38. إِنِّي الْخَدِيمِ حَيْثُ أُقِيمُ وَلَا أَرِيمُ ذَا ٱلْإِجْتِزَاءِ

39. أَنْتَ مُجِيرِي مِنَ ٱلْغَرُورِ وَ مِنْ غُرُورِ دَاعِي شَقَاءِ
40. صُنتَ مَكَانِي زِدتَّ أَمَانِي هَبْ لِي زَمَانِي بِذِي الْبَقَاءِ

41. أَنْتَ سُلُوكِي إِلَى ٱلْمَلِيكِ مَاحِي الْأُفُوكِ مُعْطِي النَّقَاءِ
42. أَنْتَ ٱلْجَمِيلُ لَكَ أَمِيلُ أَنْتَ الرَّسُولُ بِلَا جِرَاءِ

43. *For You my tongue, with my spirit, not poetic flattery, but with sincerity.*
44. *You are the road, by You the Homecoming, to He who grants the best prosperity.*

45. *You hid my nudity, rid my anxiety, granted surety, as with the Great.*
46. *O Best in Creation! Without blame or misgiving, to You my pen I consecrate.*

47. *Your deeds are beauty. Yours are the virtues. You are the means to Him of the Decree*
48. *In You my Serenity, my way to the Mighty, free from strife, for eternity.*

49. *Best of Servants! Gateway to benefits, light of all lands, my sublime aspiration*
50. *You rid me of anguish and of blemish. Grant me knowledge leading to salvation.*

51. *You rid me of poverty and kept my secrets, without deceit or calumny.*
52. *You cleansed my soul, freed me from my cell, and lifted my veil of uncertainty.*

53. *You sheltered me, and my vicinities. You honed my talents with benevolence.*
54. *For You my return, among my communities, saved from hunger and misguidance.*

55. *Yours are the blessings. I turn toward You, after my prayers, with eulogies.*[24]
56. *I'm pleased with You. You satisfy me. Through You I've forgotten my difficulties.*

57. *For You my praises. Yours is the righteousness. Yours is the success. Yours is the prize!*
58. *In Your name I call out to all the lands: Come serve your Maker, Master of the skies!*[25]

59. *In You I'm erasing any transgressions, seeking in You the greatest bounty.*
60. *In coming or going, from You never roaming, to You I pledge my loyalty.*

61. *You rid me of vice, placing all those around me, beyond the pall of murk and gloom.*
62. *Best of effacers! You purged my sins, and the frivolities of my days in bloom.*

63. *You are my Beloved, You who are loved through me, with no affront, and faultlessly.*
64. *You the most heedful, the best of pastors, best in summoning to the Heavenly*

65. *Blessings upon You, and those around You, from He who threw, when the lances flew.*[26]
66. *Upon You peace, along with honor, from He who glorifies the Elect through You.*

67. *You who reign supreme among the Chosen, By You I direct, beneficently*
68. *Those with intellect, on the Messenger's path, erasing neglect and mystery.*[27]

69. *For the intelligent He is resplendent, erasing error and insolence.*
70. *This is the obeyed, the valiant and brave, fearsome to those in disobedience.*

71. *This is the favored friend, close confidant, most preferred, provided with purity.*
72. *This is the prestigious, esteemed and prodigious, illustrious for his charity.*

73. *A priceless treasure, precious beyond all measure, Prince is He, among the Prophets.*
74. *Sun of suns, Prince of Princes, to the Saints an ally and dearest of intimates.*

43. لَكَ لِسَانِي مَعَ ٱلْجَنَانِ وَلَا أُدَانِي كَالشُّعَرَاءِ
44. أَنْتَ السَّبِيلُ بِكَ الْوُصُولُ لِمَنْ يُّنِيلُ خَيْرَ ثَرَاءِ

45. أَذْهَبْتَ عُرْيِي أَذْهَبْتَ غَيِّي كَمَّلْتَ رَعْيِي كَالْكُبَرَاءِ
46. خَيْرَ ٱلْأَنَامِ فِيكَ قِلَامِي بِلَا مَلَامِ بَلْ بِرِضَاءِ

47. يَا ذَا ٱلْجَمِيلَةْ يَا ذَا ٱلْفَضِيلَةْ أَنْتَ ٱلْوَسِيلَةْ لِذِي ٱلْقَضَاءِ
48. فِيكَ سُكُونِي إِلَى ٱلْمَتِينِ بِلَا فُتُونِ وَلَا انْقِضَاءِ

49. خَيْرَ ٱلْعِبَادِ بَابَ الْأَيَادِ نُورَ ٱلْبِلَادِ أَسْنَى رَجَاءِ
50. أَذْهَبْتَ غَمِّي مَحَوْتَ ظُلْمِي لِي جُدْ بِعِلْمِ دَاعِي نَجَاءِ

51. أَذْهَبْتَ فَقْرِي لِي صُنْتَ سِرِّي مِنْ غَيْرِ مَكْرِ وَلَا هِجَاءِ
52. زَكَّيْتَ نَفْسِي فَكَكْتَ حَبْسِي أَذْهَبْتَ لَبْسِي ذُدْتَّ غِطَائِي

53. صُنْتَ جِهَاتِي زِدْتَّ هِبَاتِي أَبْقَيْتَ ذَاتِي مَعَ ٱلْعَطَاءِ
54. لَكَ رُجُوعِي مَعَ جُمُوعِي بِغَيْرِ جُوعِي وَلَا خَطَاءِ

55. لَكَ ٱلْتِفَاتِي يَا ذَا الصِّلَاتِ بَعْدَ صَلَاتِي مَعَ الثَّنَاءِ
56. عَنْكَ رَضِيتُ بِكَ نَسِيتُ كَمَا غَنِيتُ عَنِ ٱلْعَنَاءِ

57. لَكَ امْتِدَاحِي يَا ذَا الصَّلَاحِ يَا ذَا ٱلْفَلَاحِ يَا ذَا ٱلْغِنَاءِ
58. فِيكَ أُنَادِي كُلَّ ٱلْبِلَادِ لِذِي ٱلْعِبَادِ بَانِي ٱلْغِمَاءِ

59. فِيكَ مَحَوْتُ مَا قَدْ جَنَيْتُ فِيكَ ابْتَغَيْتُ خَيْرَ نَمَاءِ
60. فِيكَ ذَهَابِي فِيكَ إِيَابِي بِلَا اغْتِرَابِي لَكَ انْتِمَاءِ

61. زَحْزَحْتَ عَابِي حُطْتَّ جَنَابِي بِلَا كَئَابِي وَلَا هَبَاءِ
62. يَا خَيْرَ مَاحِي مَحَا جُنَاحِي مَعَ ٱلْمِزَاحِ وَقْتَ الصِّبَاءِ

63. أَنْتَ حَبِيبِي يَا مَنْ حُبِّي بِي بِلَا عُيُوبِ وَلَا سِبَاءِ
64. يَا خَيْرَ وَاعِ يَا خَيْرَ رَاعِ يَا خَيْرَ دَاعِ لِذِي السَّمَاءِ

65. صَلَّى عَلَيْكَ بِمَنْ لَّدَيْكَ مُثْنٍ عَلَيْكَ عِنْدَ الرِّمَاءِ
66. عَلَيْكَ سَلَّمْ دَأْبًا وَكَرَّمْ مَنْ بِكَ عَظَّمْ أَهْلَ اعْتِمَاءِ

67. بِكَ أَقُودُ بِكَ أُفِيدُ يَا مَنْ يَّسُودُ ذَوِي اصْطِفَاءِ
68. ذَوِي ٱلْعُقُولِ نَهْجَ الرَّسُولِ مَاحِي ٱلْغُفُولِ مَاحِي ٱلْخَفَاءِ

69. ذَوِي الذَّكَاءِ لِذِي ٱلْبَهَاءِ مَاحِي ٱلْخَطَاءِ مَاحِي ٱلْجَفَاءِ
70. ذَاكَ ٱلْمُطَاعُ ذَاكَ الشُّجَاعُ بِهِ يُرَاعُ ذَوِي ٱلْإِبَاءِ

71. ذَاكَ ٱلْوَلِيُّ ذَاكَ النَّجِيُّ ذَاكَ الصَّفِيُّ ذُو ٱلْإِجْتِبَاءِ
72. ذَاكَ ٱلْحِسِيبُ ذَاكَ النَّسِيبُ ذَاكَ ٱلْعَجِيبُ بَادِي ٱلْحِبَاءِ

73. وَهْوَ النَّفِيسُ فَلَا تَقِيسُوا وَهْوَ الرَّئِيسُ لِلْأَنْبِيَاءِ
74. شَمْسُ الشُّمُوسِ رَأْسُ الرُّءُوسِ خَيْرُ ٱلْأَنِيسِ لِلْأَوْلِيَاءِ

75. *Healer of hearts, the glow of the hearths, the fullest of moons, shining luminously.*
76. *Divine rain to the grateful, lion to the hateful, and the unfaithful and cowardly.*

77. *Garden of the guided, fire of the misled, eminence clear to those who reflect*
78. *Eraser of error, bearer of gifts, for creation a guide without defect*

79. *For Him is distinction, and intercession, primacy for His communities.*[28]
80. *And if one desires knowledge, another fortune, and a third incites hostilities . . .*

81. *The one will be guided, the other sufficed, woe to the third, expelled for his spite!*
82. *He is guide and guardian, luminous light, heavenly herald, guiding aright.*

83. *He of the summons, He of the sight, is aid and safety, but warns rebels fiercely*
84. *Healing afflictions, fulfilling petitions, He listens closely to every plea.*

85. *Sanctuary of votaries, and wayfarers, for the Godly, He lights the darkness*
86. *He mends the sundered, the poor, loathed and wayward. He is refuge, renown and richness*

87. *He is the seen, and the concealed, close confidant of the Lord of Eternity.*
88. *For Him the address, and the response, for Him satisfaction and veracity.*[29]

89. *For Him is piety, For Him elation, and the houris of the afterlife.*
90. *To Him I speak, with introspection, after resolute repentance of all vice.*

91. *Miracles given to no one before, nor ever more, such are Your prodigies.*
92. *Including ridding awful things from the fearful, who seek recourse and remedies.*

93. *Best of Creations! You drove tribulations, off to the errant, granting salvation.*
94. *You are the Gracious. I'm the servant, endlessly devoted to your veneration.*[30]

95. *Praise welled in me, and flowed profitably, ending disgrace and difficulty.*
96. *Praise is my profit, my edifice and achievement, this I declare definitively.*

97. *But I have failed to reach my goal. I cannot equal in praise, the Nobles of old.*
98. *My ink seeps away, my mind in a daze, the Deputies' guide, I cannot extol.*

99. *For how can I sing His praises, when even the Sages, lack such ability?*
100. *So I call all servants to my pillar, though they needn't abandon home or country.*

101. *O people of land! O people of sea! Rush to the Pious, the bountiful ocean!*
102. *He washed away my faults, revealed the concealed, and cleansed my heart of imperfection.*

103. *Channel of benefits, slayer of enemies, He met my needs abundantly.*
104. *Forging virtues from vices, He mends homes in crisis, or aftermath of tragedy.*

105. *What a heart! What a friend! What a mind! The end of mystery, no need to wonder!*
106. *He saved the people, absolved us from battle, the end of exile, no need to wander!*[31]

75. شِفَا الصُّدُورِ ضِيَاءُ الدُّورِ بَدْرُ ٱلْبُدُورِ بَادِي الضِّيَاءِ
76. غَيْثُ شَكُورٍ لَيْثُ كَفُورٍ نَافِي نَفُورٍ مُبْدِي قِلَاءِ

77. جَنَّاتُ هَادِي نِيرَانُ عَادِ فَٱلْفَضْلُ بَادِي لِلْعُقَلَاءِ
78. مَاحِي ٱلْخَطَايَا بَادِي ٱلْعَطَايَا هَادِي ٱلْبَرَايَا بِلَا غَلَاءِ

79. لَهُ ٱلْبَرَاعَةْ لَهُ الشَّفَاعَةْ لَهُ جَمَاعَةْ حَاوِي ارْتِقَاءِ
80. إِنْ رَّامَ عِلْمًا أَوْ رَامَ غُنْمًا أَوْ رَامَ ظُلْمًا بَاغِي الِّلقَاءِ

81. فَذَاكَ يُهْدَى وَذَاكَ يُهْدَى لَهُ وَيُرْدَى ذَا بِشَقَاءِ
82. هَادٍ مُجِيرُ نُورٌ مُّنِيرُ غَيْثٌ بَشِيرُ لِذِي اهْتِدَاءِ

83. حَامٍ نَّصِيرُ دَاعٍ بَّصِيرُ لَيْثٌ نَّذِيرُ لِذِي اعْتِدَاءِ
84. مُشْكٍ لِّشَاكٍ بِشْرٌ لِبَاكٍ مُصْغٍ لِحَاكٍ وَذِي نِدَاءِ

85. مُنجٍ لِّسَالِكْ مَنجًى لِّنَاسِكْ جَالِي حَوَالِكْ عَنْ ذِي اتِّقَاءِ
86. غُنْمُ فَقِيرُ جَبْرُ كَسِيرِ صِيتُ حَقِيرِ بَاقِي وِقَاءِ

87. وَهْوَ ٱلْجَلِيُّ وَهْوَ ٱلْخَفِيُّ وَهْوَ النَّجِيُّ لِذِي ٱلْبَقَاءِ
88. لَهُ ٱلْخِطَابُ لَهُ ٱلْجَوَابُ لَهُ الصَّوَابُ مَعَ الرِّضَاءِ

89. لَهُ ٱلْبُرُورُ لَهُ السُّرُورُ تَلْقَاهُ حُورُ بَعْدَ ٱلْقَضَاءِ
90. لَهُ خِطَابِي بَعْدَ مَتَابِي مِنْ كُلِّ عَابِ مَعَ ٱلْمَضَاءِ

91. لَكَ خَوَارِقْ مِنْ ذِي ٱلْخَلَائِقْ لَيْسَتْ لِسَابِقْ وَلَا لِجَاءِ
92. مِنْهَا انْصِرَافُ شَيٍّ يُعَافُ عَمَّنْ يَخَافُ بَعْدَٱلْتِجَاءِ

93. خَيْرَ ٱلْبَرَايَا ذُدْتَّ ٱلْبَلَايَا لِذِي ٱلْخَطَايَا رُمْتَ نَجَاءِ
94. أَنْتَ ٱلْكَرِيمُ أَنَا ٱلْخَدِيمُ دَهْرًا أُدِيمُ فِيكَ ثَنَاءِ

95. رُمْتُ امْتِدَاحَا يُعْطِي فَلَاحَا يَكْفِي افْتِضَاحَا مَعَ ٱلْعَنَاءِ
96. إِنِّي بِمَدْحِي عَايَنْتُ رِبْحِي قَطْعًا وَنُجْحِي مَعَ ٱلْبِنَاءِ

97. لَكِنْ عَجَزْتُ عَمَّا ٱلْتَمَسْتُ وَمَا مَدَحْتُ كَالنُّبَلَاءِ
98. غَارَ مِدَادِي حَارَ فُؤَادِي عَنْ مَّدْحِ هَادِي لِلْبُدَلَاءِ

99. فَكَيْفَ أَحْوِي مَدْحًا لِمُحْيِ وَٱلْمَدْحُ مُعْيِ لِلْعُقَلَاءِ
100. لَكِنْ أُنَادِي كُلَّ ٱلْبِلَادِ إِلَى عِمَادِي بِلَا جَلَاءِ

101. يَا أَهْلَ بَرٍّ يَا أَهْلَ بَحْرِ عُوجُواْ لِبَرٍّ بَحْرِ السَّخَاءِ
102. مَاحِي عُيُوبِي مُبْدِي غُيُوبِي مُنْقِي جُيُوبِي مِنَ الطَّخَاءِ

103. مُسْدِي أَيَادِي مُرْدِي أَعَادِي مُعْطِي مُرَادِي مَعَ الرَّخَاءِ
104. مَاحِي الرَّذَائِلْ مُعْطِي الْفَضَائِلْ مُحْيِي الْمَنَازِلْ بَعْدَ الْعَفَاءِ

105. نِعْمْ الْحَبِيبُ نِعْمَ الْقَرِيبِ نِعْمَ اللَّبِيبُ مَاحِي الْخَفَاءِ
106. حَمَى الْعِيَالَا كَفَى الْقِتَالَا مَحَى الْمَجَالَا بِلَا رِفَاءِ

107. *Righting wickedness, showing kindness, He gives joy to all who hope expectantly.*
108. *He heals the ailing, and the aching. He ends the suffering, leading servants to Safety.*

109. *Shattering shackles and showering favors, danger is gone, beneficence has come!*
110. *Ravage is over and marvels revealed, the end of ordeals, by the Munificent One!*

111. *He guides goodness to our residence. His aid in evidence in its resplendency.*[32]
112. *Heaven-sent, to those seeking benefit, fierce as a lion to treacherous enemies*

113. *For Him the feats, for Him the marvels, for Him the wonders, without any limit.*
114. *A gazelle speaks to Him, a lizard salutes Him, a bird sings praises, as if sentient.*

115. *A well overflowed without pail or rope! A tree walked by His leave! God's rain gushed in sheets!*
116. *A tree stump adored Him, and cried out for Him! A wolf, turned shepherd, tended the sheep!*

117. *He gained His glory on the Midnight Journey, not in fantasy, but in the flesh.*
118. *Glory to the Lord! Whose Beloved drew near, by night, in innocence, at His behest.*

119. *Once purified, He made the journey, bringing joy to the Prophetic Assembly.*
120. *The Trustworthy traveled, with Trusted Guide, on Trusty Steed, to peaks of purity.*[33]

121. *It erased uncertainty, showing His beauty, and magnificence, to the Pious.*
122. *They gave Him precedence, and due reverence, raised to eminence by the Flawless.*

123. *And He is Lord of them. He stands out above them. His Ascension brought ascendancy.*
124. *That night He returned, and favors poured forth, from the Everlasting, flowing abundantly.*

125. *For the Good, He returned with provisions, but for the wicked, woe and afflictions.*
126. *He gained perfection, and through election, was raised above men of distinction.*

127. *Favored with majesty, and with beauty, from our Lord, the Exalted and Heavenly*
128. *Shield of my kin, sentinel of men, citadel of women, glory to the Lofty!*

129. *O How Glorious! O How Gracious! Indeed among princes, He is principal.*
130. *He halts the Deceiver, ends deception, accepts devotion, forever mindful.*

131. *He raises dwellings, fills them with blessings, assuring joy for His assemblies.*
132. *For Him my tributes, after my triumphs, over my trials, daily and nightly.*[34]

133. *Six in prayers, and Six in praises, conveyed Him unfailingly, throughout the year.*
134. *Upon Him Blessings, the Lord did raise Him. Among the Pious He has no peer.*[35]

135. *Upon Him Peace! Reward His greatness! Among the Sages, proclaim His Excellency!*
136. *Upon the Venerable, all contentment, gate of the path, His brother in certainty.*[36]

137. *Upon the Vizier, guard of the Decree, the Herald's sword, the Almighty's pleasure.*[37]
138. *On the Vivid and Virtuous, may our Timeless Lord, grant accord, in fullest measure.*[38]

107. أَخْفَى الشُّرُورَا أَبْدَى الْخُيُورَا قَادَ السُّرُورَا لِذِي الرَّجَاءِ
108. شَفَى السَّقِيمَا نَفَى الْأَلِيمَا قَادَ الْخَدِيمَا إِلَى النَّجَاءِ

109. قَدْ فَكَّ كَبْلَا قَدْ بَثَّ فَضْلَا فَالضُّرُّ وَلَّا وَالنَّفْعُ جَاءِ
110. جَالِي النَّوَائِبْ مُبْدِي عَجَائِبْ نَافِي مَصَائِبْ بَادِي الُّلهَاءِ

111. مُسْدِي الْخُيُورِ إِلَى الْقُصُورِ بَادِي النُّصُورِ بَادِي ٱلْبَهَاءِ
112. غَيْثٌ أَفَادَا مَنِ اسْتَفَادَا لَيْثٌ أَبَادَا عِدَى الدَّهَاءِ

113. لَهُ مَنَاقِبْ لَهُ عَجَائِبْ لَهُ غَرَائِبْ بِلَا انْتِهَاءِ
114. ظَبْيٌ يُّكَلِّمْ ضَبٌّ يُّسَلِّمْ طَيْرٌ يُّعَظِّمْ كَذِي دَهَاءِ

115. سَرْحٌ تَسِيرُ غَيْثٌ يَفُورُ بِيرٌ تَفُورُ بِلَا رِشَاءِ
116. جِذْعٌ يَحِنُّ لَهُ يَئِنُّ ذِيبٌ يَعِنُّ بِرَعْيِ شَاءِ

117. قَدْ حَازَ فَخْرَا مِنْ حِينَ أَسْرَى بِالْجِسْمِ جَهْرَا بِلَا افْتِرَاءِ
118. أَكْرِمْ بِرَبٍّ أَسْرَى بِحِبٍّ لَيْلًا لِّقُرْبٍ مَعَ الْبَرَاءِ

119. قَدْ بَاتَ يَسْرِي مِنْ بَعْدِ طُهْرِ مُدِيمَ بِشْرِ فِي الْأَنْبِيَاءِ
120. سُرَى الْأَمِينِ مَعَ الْأَمِينِ فَوْقَ الْأَمِينِ لِلْأَصْفِيَاءِ

121. مَحَى الضَّلَالَا أَبْدَى الْجَلَالَا أَبْدَى الْجَمَالَا لِلْأَتْقِيَاءِ
122. قَدْ قَدَّمُوهُ إِذْ وَاجَهُوهُ وَاحْتَرَمُوهُ ذَوِي نَقَاءِ

123. وَسَادَ فِيهِمْ وَبَانَ عَنْهُمْ وَصِينَ عَنْهُمْ بَعْدَ ارْتِقَاءِ
124. قَدْ آبَ لَيْلَا قَدْ صَبَّ نَيْلَا قَدْ فَاقَ سَيْلَا مِنْ ذِي الْبَقَاءِ

125. قَدْ جَا بِمَيْرِ لِأَهْلِ خَيْرِ وَبَا بِضَيْرِ أَهْلِ الشَّقَاءِ
126. حَازَ الْكَمَالَا فَاقَ الرِّجَالَا جَازَ الْمَجَالَا بِالْإِعْتِمَاءِ

127. نَالَ جَلَالَا نَالَ جَمَالَا مِمَّنْ تَعَالَى رَبِّ السَّمَاءِ
128. أَكْرِمْ بِعَالِ حَامِي عِيَالِي رَاعِي الرِّجَالِ حِصْنِ النِّسَاءِ

129. نِعْمَ الْعَظِيمُ نِعْمَ ٱلْكَرِيمُ نِعْمَ ٱلْمُقِيمُ لِلرُّؤَسَاءِ
130. كَافِي الْغَرُورِ مَاحِي الْغُرُورِ مُعْطِي الْبُرُورِ بِلَا نَسَاءِ

131. بَانِي الدُّيُورِ مَعَ الْخُيُورِ بَاغِي السُّرُورِ لِلْجُلَسَاءِ
132. لَهُ امْتِدَاحِي بَعْدَ نَجَاحِي عِنْدَ الصَّبَاحِ وَفِي الْمَسَاءِ

133. صَلَاةُ سِتَّةْ بِمَدْحِ سِتَّةْ تَأْتِيهِ بَتَّهْ مَعَ ائْتِسَاءِ
134. عَلَيْهِ صَلَّى رَبٌّ أَجَلَّا فَفَاقَ الْكُلَّا بِالْأَتْقِيَاءِ

135. عَلَيْهِ سَلَّمْ وَالْأَمْرَ فَخَّمْ وَالْأَجْرَ عَظَّمْ فِي الْأَذْكِيَاءِ
136. عَلَى الْعَتِيقِ بَابِ الطَّرِيقِ أَخِي الْوُثُوقِ كُلُّ رِضَاءِ

137. عَلَى الْوَزِيرِ سَيْفِ الْبَشِيرِ رِضَى الْقَدِيرِ مُجْرِي الْقَضَاءِ
138. عَلَى الضِّيَاءِ أَخِي الْحَيَاءِ خَيْرُ رِضَاءِ مِنْ ذِي ٱلْبَقَاءِ

139. *Upon the Near and Dear, the Lion of War, may He Who Answers grant ascendancy.*[39]
140. *Upon the Cohort, who answered the call in darkest hours, His honor and clemency.*

141. *In troubled times, they were victor and vanquished, theirs is dignity, O Such Men!*
142. *On the day of Humility, the day of Appeals, May He Who Hears, be pleased with them.*

143. *Founts of good for seekers of gain, sources of pain for seekers of hostilities*
144. *They rose to the occasion, in confrontation, full of bravery and loyalty.*

145. *Such gallant knights! Such brave defenders! Slaying antagonists without cowardice.*
146. *By their grace I've forgiven, without malice, by them I've banished the slanderous.*

147. *Divert my foes, avert all harm, by the kind listener, who rids of tyranny.*
148. *I entrust my affairs, to Him my renewer, and those at Badr, with certainty.*[40]

149. *So again I pray, please turn away, those who come to me, bearing their oppression.*
150. *O Lord of Majesty, Exalted Master, O Dearest Friend, grant this supplication!*

151. *Prayers and Peace, on the guard of my hearths, keeper of my heart, who spoke with the Heavenly.*
152. *Upon the Messenger, the watchful shepherd, gateway to He who fulfills the plea . . .*

153. *Unending Blessing and increasing Peace. Grant my words and actions Your acceptance.*[41]
154. *Lord of Volition, source of all gain, sustain my happiness! Grant me abundance!*

155. *Keep me from evils, strengthen my morals, by His example, and effortlessly.*
156. *Bless my sustenance, daily and nightly. Keep my passing free of antipathy.*

157. *O Lord of Existence! Please be generous! Raise my night vigils high aloft.*
158. *Lavish love upon me! Fulfill my longing, You whose benefits are without cost.*

159. *Grant me devotion, save me from illusion, make my worship a joy for all who see.*
160. *Please accept my pen. Please approve my words. Free them from blame and all controversy.*

161. *Untie my tongue. Enhance my surety. Refine my purity. Enlighten my spirit.*
162. *You dispelled the threat. You met my needs. Spare me the iniquity of the cynic.*

163. *Save my dependents from misguidance. And from the licit, sustain my prosperity.*
164. *Lord of the Covenant, grant Your Book to me. Accept my penance. Guard my dignity.*

165. *O Best of Lords, most nurturing Master, You soothed my heart and trained my spirit.*
166. *Prayers and Peace on Him, He fulfilled Your mission, and grant me salvation, without limit.*

O My Dear God! By the Face of God Most High, the Gracious!
Blessings, Peace, and Grace upon our lord and master Muhammad and His family and companions.
And bring joy to Him with these rhymes in every hour and every age for all eternity!

139. عَلَى الْقَرِيبِ لَيْثِ الْحُرُوبِ رِضَى الْمُجِيبِ مَعَ ارْتِقَاءِ
140. عَلَى الصَّحَابَهْ ذَوِي الْإِجَابَهْ يَوْمَ الْكَئَابَهْ رِضَى الثَّنَاءِ

141. نِعْمَ الرِّجَالُ لَهُمْ مَجَالُ نِيلُواْ وَنَالُواْ وَقْتَ الْعَنَاءِ
142. رِضَى السَّمِيعِ عَلَى الْجَمِيعِ يَوْمَ الْخُشُوعِ يَوْمَ النِّدَاءِ

143. أَرْبَابِ خَيْرِ أَرْبَابِ ضَيْرِ لِبَاغِي مَيْرِ أَوِ اعْتِدَاءِ
144. كُلٌّ شُجَاعُ لَهُ اتِّبَاعُ لَهُ ارْتِفَاعُ وَقْتَ الرِّفَاءِ

145. نِعْمَ الْكُمَاةُ نِعْمَ الْحُمَاةُ عِدًى أَمَاتُوا بِلَا اخْتِفَاءِ
146. بِهِمْ عَفَوْتُ وَمَا جَفَوْتُ بِهِمْ نَفَيْتُ ذَوِي افْتِرَاءِ

147. تَنْحُو لِغَيْرِي أَعْدَاءُ ضَيْرِ بِأُذْنِ خَيْرِ مَاحِي اجْتِرَاءِ
148. فَوَّضْتُ أَمْرِي لِمُبْقِي عُمْرِي مَعَ اهْلِ بَدْرِ بِلَا امْتِرَاءِ

149. إِنِّي أَقُولُ وَلَا يَمِيلُ لِي مَنْ يَّصُولُ مَعَ الْجِرَاءِ
150. يَا ذَا الْجَلَالِ يَا مُتَعَالِ يَا خَيْرَ وَالِ أَجِبْ دُعَاءِ

151. صَلِّ وَسَلِّمْ عَلَى الْمُكَلِّمْ وَ دُورِيَ اعْصِمْ وَصُنْ وِعَاءِ
152. عَلَى الرَّسُولِ بَابِ الْوُصُولِ لِنَيْلِ سُولِ أَحْمَى رُعَائِي

153. صَلِّ دَوَامًا وَ زِدْ سَلَامَا وَاشْكُرْ قِلَامَا لِي وَبِنَائِي
154. يَا ذَا الْإِرَادَةْ يَا ذَا الْإِفَادَةْ خَلِّدْ سَعَادَةْ لِي بِاعْتِنَاءِ

155. قِنِي اعْتِدَاءَا زِدْنِي اهْتِدَاءَا زِدْنِي اقْتِدَاءَا بِلَا عَنَاءِ
156. صَفِّ اخْتِفَاءِ بِلَا جَفَاءِ طَيِّبْ عَشَائِي طَيِّبْ غَدَائِي

157. يَا ذَا الْوُجُودِ كُنْ لِي بِجُودِ وَاجْعَلْ هُجُودِي فَوْقَ الْأَدَاءِ
158. هَبْ لِي وِدَادَا قُدْ لِي الْمُرَادَا يَا مَنْ أَفَادَا بِلَا كِرَاءِ

159. هَبْ لِي بُرُورَا قِنِي الْغَرُورَا عَبْدًا سُرُورَا لِكُلِّ رَاءِ
160. وَاشْكُرْ قِلَامِي وَاحْمَدْ كَلَامِي بِلَا مَلَامِي وَلَا امْتِرَاءِ

161. سَدِّدْ لِسَانِي نَوِّرْ جَنَانِي صَفِّ أَمَانِي وَزِدْ بَرَائِي
162. زَحْزَحْتَ ضَيْرَا لِي قُدْتَّ مَيْرَا فَلْتَكْفِ جَوْرَا لِي مَنْ يُّرَائِي

163. أَنْقِذْ عِيَالِي مِنَ الضَّلَالِ وَبِالْحَلَالِ خَلِّدْ ثَرَاءِ
164. قِنِي عِتَابَا قُدْ لِي الْكِتَابَا وَاقْبَلْ مَتَابَا يَا ذَا اشْتِرَاءِ

165. يَا خَيْرَ رَبٍّ خَيْرَ مُرَبٍّ طَيَّبْتَ قَلْبِي بَعْدَ اجْتِدَاءِ
166. صَلِّ وَسَلِّمْ عَلَى الْمُتَمِّمْ وَكُلِّيَ اعْصِمْ بِلَا انْتِهَاءِ

اللَّهُمَّ صَلِّ وَسَلِّمْ وَبَارِكْ عَلَى سَيِّدِنَا وَمَوْلَانَا مُحَمَّدٍ وَآلِهِ وَصَحْبِهِ وَفَرِّحْهُ بِهَذِهِ الْمَنْظُومَةِ فِي كُلِّ وَقْتٍ وَحِينٍ أَبَدًا وَهَبْ لِنَاظِمِهَا رِضَاكَ الْأَكْبَرِ فِي كُلِّ حَرْفٍ مِنْهَا وَهَبْ لِكُلِّ مَنْ يَّقْرَأُهَا سَعَادَةَ الدَّارَيْنِ آمِينْ يَّا رَبَّ الْعَالَمِينَ.
سُبْحَانَ رَبِّكَ رَبِّ الْعِزَّةِ عَمَّا يَصِفُونَ وَ سَلَامٌ عَلَى الْمُرْسَلِينَ وَالْحَمْدُ لِلَّهِ رَبِّ الْعَالَمِينَ.

Notes

[13] This is the *salāt al-fātih,* a centuries-old prayer on the Prophet that is widely employed, but in Africa is particularly associated with the Tijaniyya. It is worth noting that Bamba openly lauds Aḥmad al-Tijānī and the litanies of the Tijāniyya (which he employed before establishing the Murīdiyya) in a number of works, including *Masālik al-Jinān.*

[14] *Imān, Islām,* and *Iḥsān.* Bamba, who often puts the emphasis on understanding before action, employs this arrangement of the basic elements of Islam drawn from the *Iḥyāʾ ʿulūm al-Dīn* by Abū Ḥāmid b. Muḥammad al-Ghazālī (1058–1111 CE) rather than the more common *islām, imān,* and *iḥsān* configuration from most familiar renderings of the hadith of Gabriel.

[15] Here, as in verse 89 below, the reference to *houris* is to the innocent companions promised to the inhabitants of Paradise in the Qurʾan. The preamble and epilogue give remarkable insight into Bamba's intentions in writing the poem, as well as the great importance Murids place on reciting it.

[16] *minhu fidāʾī. From him is my redemption:* he redeemed me, he released me. The juxtaposition of this line about redemption with the next line, which alludes to imprisonment and release, makes it clear that he is referring to his deportation and exile to Gabon from 1895 to 1902. However, I think the poem is meant to allude to both spiritual and bodily emancipation granted by God and the Prophet. The enemies that he is referring to repeatedly in this poem can obviously be read as referring to the French (and African chiefs) who conspired to have him arrested without cause and exiled, but he is also clearly referring in places to the four principal enemies discussed in the *Masālik* and many other classical texts, the lower soul, the devil, the passions, and the world. In Arabic these are *nafs, shayṭān, hawā,* and *dunyā,* and in the teaching of the Murīdiyya they are recalled with the mnemonic device *na-sha-ha-du,* "we bear witness."

[17] I have interpreted these freely for meaning and effect. More literally they would be: *For you my pleasure, for you my honor, for you my dependence, with my urgent plea—you who healed me, you who shielded me, from he who oppressed me, by cleansing me of malady.*

[18] In verses 6–7 and again in verse 11, Bamba appears to refer to the visionary experiences of the author of the most famous piece of Sufi *madḥa,* the famed *Qasīdat al-Burda* by Muḥammad b. Saʿīd al-Būṣīrī (d. 1296). Bamba uses constructions that seem to allude to the Shādhilī Sufi's claim that he wrote the poem in hopes of recovering from a grave illness: "I was suddenly paralysed [*sic*] down one side of my body by a stroke. I decided to compose this ode, the Burdah. I hoped that it would be a means unto Allah, by which he would cure me. So I recited it again and again, weeping, praying, and petitioning God. I fell asleep, and in a dream, I saw the Blessed Prophet. He moved his noble hand across my face, and placed his cloak upon me. When I awoke, I found that I had recovered my health." Bamba's lines here seem to draw a parallel between the crippling illness that Busiri faced and the devastating oppression of forced exile and imprisonment. The Prophet visits Būṣīrī and heals him of his illness after his fervent prayers and supplications. Bamba is released from oppression after seven years of imprisonment. His visionary experiences with the Prophet have—like Būṣīrī—seen him through his ordeal. His prayers have been answered. It is worth noting that before founding the Murīdiyya, Bamba routinely employed Shādhilī ritual litanies (*awrād*) and that the Burda was and is widely read in West Africa. For an excellent translation alongside the Arabic original, see Stefan Sperl and Christopher Shackle, *Qasida Poetry in Islamic Asia and Africa,* vol. 2 (Leiden: Brill, 1996), 388–412. For the quotation above, see Syed Mohiuddin Qadri, *Qasidat al-Burdah: The Poem of the Mantle* (San Francisco:

Creative Commons, 2008), 7, http://www.scribd.com/doc/41950068/Qasida-Burda-Shareef-by-Imam-Busairi.

[19] This is *wāli,* usually meaning patron, rather than *walī,* usually meaning friend or saint (friend of God). These are distinct (though related) technical terms in Sufism, so eliding them a bit in the sense of "protecting friend" seems to provide both an echo of the original and a rhyme.

[20] "State" would be a more literal option here instead of "station," since the former is often used to translate *ḥāl* and the latter often used to translate *maqām.*

[21] Here, Bamba begins to shift his address from God to the Prophet, referring to him in third person until turning to address him in second person in verse 33.

[22] Verse 39 alludes obliquely to the idea, expressed in a number of hadith reports, that the *shayṭān* cannot take the form of the Prophet. This seems directly connected to verse 40, which refers to the visionary experiences Bamba had of the Prophet in Touba during Ramadan 1312 AH (March 1895), wherein the Prophet assured him that he would be made the *quṭb al-zamān,* the pole of the era. ʿAbdul-Aḥad Mbacké (1914–1989), one of Bamba's sons and the third caliph in the Murīdiyya, gave many accounts of this visionary experience orally and at least one written account in 1979 in Arabic. Moustapha Diakhaté has a French-language account of the visionary experience, *L'exil de Khadimou Rassoul,* based mainly on Caliph ʿAbdul-Aḥad's account as well as that of Moussa Ka. I have not been able to find a copy of this short book in North America, so some of what I present here is based on the author's, Diakhaté's, reading of the book in Wolof for a Murid informational website. I accessed it in April and May of 2013 at http://www.youtube.com/watch?v=4I0ZT766m70.

[23] The term translated here as "path" is *sulūk,* which has technical connotations of "wayfaring" in the Sufi tradition. The term appears again in a different form in verse 85.

[24] *ṣilāt,* gifts, is the first part of the line, but the reference is clearly to *ṣalāt ʿala al-nābī,* prayers of peace on the Prophet, and there is a play on words with *ṣilāt* and *ṣalāt,* so "blessings" is the most appropriate translation for "gifts" here. Incidentally, there is an error in the Arabic transcription of this line in the Sam Mbaye edition of this text in *Diwān fī amdāḥ khayr al-mursalīn;* both words are rendered as *ṣalāt.*

[25] This line is more literally, come serve your Master, Maker of the skies; however, reversing the nouns makes the line work much better in English without violating the basic meaning.

[26] A reference to Qurʾan 8:17.

[27] Bamba moves from second-person address of the Prophet back to third person here.

[28] It becomes clear throughout the poem that the Prophetic intercession that Bamba is evoking in the title is not only meant to refer to the day of judgment (as it appears to be in this verse) but rather to the Prophet's intervention, by divine permission, into the life of the saints (*awliyāʾ*).

[29] This appears to be a reference to the face-to-face conversation between Muhammad and God at the pinnacle of the *miʿrāj,* where the Prophet was brought to within two finger spans of the Divine Essence.

[30] After his visionary experiences with the Prophet (according to some accounts, these began in 1883 CE after the death of Bamba's father, Momar Anta Saly), Bamba began referring to himself as the *khadīm al-rasūl,* the servant of the Messenger. His service, his labor for the Prophet, is usually understood by Murids to mean extending the Prophet's call to Islam, singing his praises, and especially writing praise poetry.

[31] The absolution from jihad is central to Bamba's overall nonviolent thought and it is rooted in his visionary experience in Touba in 1895 before being sent into exile. During

that encounter, he saw the Prophet with his companions that fought at the famous battle of Badr in the second year of the hegira (624 CE) and asked how he could join their illustrious company. He was told that the time for spilling blood was over, but that if he wished to be raised into their company he would have to go face his enemies in his time as the people of Badr had faced theirs. According to internal Murid sources, Bamba completed his fast and went to Mbacké-Bari in Jolof, where he was arrested and later deported.

[32] The word I have translated here as residences is literally castles or palaces. It seems clear to me that Bamba is writing of Touba here, the city that he founded and wherein he reported visionary experiences with the Prophet during spiritual retreat in the mosque during the last ten days of Ramadan in 1312 AH (March 1895) that presaged his exile. But this line in its literal form is more generic and could quite easily be represented as: *He guides goodness to residences, His aid in evidence, and His resplendency.*

[33] This is all the same word, *al-Amīn;* the verbs and prepositions used make it clear that the first refers to the Prophet, the second to Jibrīl, and the third to al-Burāq, the creature that carried the Prophet on the *miʿrāj*. The verses from 117 to 126 are a pithy poetic account of the Night Journey, alluding to the Prophet Muhammad leading the congregational prayer in a gathering of all the prophets and returning confirmed in his mission. In Muslim conventional accounts, the form and number of the daily *ṣalāt* is established during the *miʿrāj,* and part of what is recited silently in the seated position in prayer is understood to reenact the conversation between God and the Prophet on that occasion.

[34] "Over my trials" is not explicit in the text, but certainly implied, and elaborating on this point allows for alliteration in the English rendition and keeping the rhythm and syllabic structure of the original.

[35] The first line here makes denotation—the year in *ṣalāt ʿala al-nābī* and *madḥa* —of what is only connotation—six (months) and six (months) in the original. This reading is especially clear, given that the preceding verse speaks of praising by day and by night, so this is just another way of dividing time rhetorically. This is also the reading taken by his son Serigne Bachir Mbacké in *Les bienfaits de l'eternel* (Dakar: Imprimerie St. Paul, 1995). Also, throughout the poem I have translated forms of *taqwā* with forms of "godly" and "pious," and either would work equally well in English verses in the second line here.

[36] Honorifics used to refer to Abū Bakr, Islam's first caliph.

[37] Honorifics referring to ʿUmar, the second caliph.

[38] Honorifics referring to ʿUthmān, the third caliph.

[39] Honorifics referring to ʿAlī, the fourth caliph, and the Prophet's cousin.

[40] The lines from 140 to 148 appear to be a general commendation of the early soldiers of Islam, but it is important to remember that Bamba reported seeing the people of Badr repeatedly during his visionary experiences with the Prophet after Ramadan 1312 (1895 CE). Also, according to his son and caliph, ʿAbdul-Aḥad Mbacké, Bamba said that he submitted to arrest by the French because he believed firmly that this was the sacrifice required of him to join the people of Badr in their state of continuous proximity to the Prophet. This interpretation is strengthened by verses 149–150 where Bamba prays directly to God to preserve him from future imprisonment or oppression, though he has made it clear a number of times in the poem that his gratitude is "free from recrimination." He accepts that his trials were a favor from God, designed to raise his station.

[41] Literally "my pens and my constructions," this passage could easily be rendered as "writings and buildings."

BOOK REVIEWS

DOI: 10.5192/215409930402249

Christopher Wise, editor and translator, and Hala Abu Taleb, translator. *Taʾrīkh al Fattāsh: The Timbuktu Chronicles 1493–1599.* Trenton, N.J.: Africa World Press, 2011. xxvii + 320 pp. $34.95

In 1999 Professor John Hunwick published his splendid scholarly translation into English of most chapters of the Timbuktu chronicle *Taʾrīkh al-Sūdān.*[1] Since then, the need for a reliable English translation of its sister chronicle *Taʾrīkh al-fattāsh* (henceforth referred to as *TF*) has been felt ever more strongly in the Anglophone world.

But it is not only the English-speaking scholarly public who have hoped for a new translation of *TF* (ideally accompanied by a parallel new edition of its Arabic text). Important critical scholarship on *TF*'s text and historical context has been published since its classical edition and French translation by Houdas and Delafosse was first printed in 1913–1914.[2] New editions of the Arabic text of the chronicle are required in our century, and new translations of it into English and other languages, taking advantage of the new insights achieved by those critical studies.[3]

Christopher Wise and Hala Abu Taleb have now produced an English translation of *TF,* and one would wish to welcome it without reservation. Unfortunately, in its present state this is a flawed, in places misleading,

[1] J. Hunwick, *Timbuktu and the Songhay Empire: Al-Saʿdī's Taʾrīkh al-Sūdān Down to 1613 and Other Contemporary Documents* (Leiden: Brill, 1999).
[2] O. Houdas and M. Delafosse, eds. and trans., *Taʾrīkh al-fattāsh* (Paris: E. Leroux, 1913–1914; most recent reprint in one volume: Paris: Librairie d'Amérique et d'Orient Adrien Maisonneuve, 1981).
[3] Notably J. Hunwick, "Studies in the *Taʾrīkh al-Fattāsh,*" part 1, *Research Bulletin–CAD* 5, nos. 1–2 (1969): 57–65; J. Hunwick, "Studies in the *Taʾrīkh al-Fattāsh,*" part 2, *Sudanic Africa* 3 (1992): 133–48; N. Levtzion, "A Seventeenth-Century Chronicle by Ibn al-Mukhtār: A Critical Study of *Taʾrīkh al-Fattāsh,*" *Bulletin of SOAS* 34, no. 3 (1971): 571–93; Madina Ly-Tall, "Remarques sur le *Tarikh el-Fettach,*" *Bulletin de l'IFAN*, series B, 34, no. 3 (1972): 471–93.

Islamic Africa, VOL. 4, NO. 2, 2013. ISSN 2154-0993.

rendering of the chronicle. Besides, the "Introduction" to the volume fails to get to grips with a central issue, namely the politico-ideological motivations that shaped *TF*'s text in the seventeenth century. Moreover, it displays only a most superficial grasp of the forgeries inserted in that text in the nineteenth century, and fails to pinpoint them. The readers are left without editorial guidance in the matter, and will be liable to mistake the seventeenth-century text and the nineteenth-century forgeries for one single seamless text.

Though a few of the critical analyses of *TF*'s text produced in recent decades are listed in the volume's short "Bibliography," the "Introduction" displays no sign of familiarity with them. Yet, taking them into account is of course indispensable to any serious twenty-first-century translator of the chronicle.

Wise is a professor of English and comparative literature at Western Washington University, and the author of several books in his field, including some on the literature of West Africa.[4] Hala Abu Taleb is an assistant professor in the American Studies Program at the University of Jordan.[5] The dust jacket, title page, and table of contents of their joint book inform us that both writers contributed to the translation, while Wise edited the work and wrote its "Introduction." We are also informed that this is an "English translation of *the original works*[6] *in Arabic* [our italics] by Al-Hājj Mahmūd Kati." Moreover, in the introduction, Wise writes that

> the version of the *Ta'rīkh al-fattāsh* that is presented here is therefore an English translation *from both the Arabic and French texts* [our italics] first edited and translated by Houdas and Delafosse, and it *includes their extensive and detailed annotations* [our italics].

However, there is reason to doubt that either Wise or Hala Abu Taleb went back to *TF*'s Arabic text in any attentive way. Besides, their English rendering of Houdas and Delafosse's French translation of the Arabic text is

---

[4] See http://onlinefast.org/wwutoday/facstaff/publications/11239.

[5] On the American Studies Program at the University of Jordan, see http://international.ju.edu.jo/Lists/OurPrograms/DispDept_Program.aspx?ID=12&Dept=International Relations and Regional Studies&DeptName=International Relations and Regional Studies.

[6] One wonders why "works" is written in the plural, as if the translation dealt with separately identified writings of Maḥmūd Kaʿti. It does no such thing.

more than once unfaithful and sometimes downright wrong. Also, contrary to what Wise asserts, crucial annotations by Houdas and Delafosse were actually left out, or misunderstood, sometimes with disastrous results.

A brief examination of pages 88–89 of the present English translation will help to sum this up. They correspond to page 44 of *TF*'s published Arabic text, and to page 83 of Houdas and Delafosse's French translation. In footnote 2 on that page, the French translators call attention to the "bizarre" construction of the Arabic phrase الاّ ڧتله لا عالم ولا جاهل لا رجال ولا نساء.[7] Wise and Hala Abu Taleb leave this footnote out, thus failing to alert the readers (as they should have done) to this particular difficulty in the translation of the Arabic text. The phrase is part of a passage about the persecution of the Fulani by the Songhay ruler *Shī* (or *Sii,* or *Sonyi*) Ali. The whole passage was translated into French by Houdas and Delafosse as "Il n'avait pas d'ennemis qu'il haïssait aussi vivement que les Peuls et ne pouvait voir un Peul <u>sans le tuer quel qu'il fût, savant ou ignorant, homme ou femme.</u>" (We have underlined the words which correspond to the Arabic quoted in Houdas and Delafosse's footnote 2.) Taking into account the whole Arabic passage in which these words are embedded, the final sentence could be rendered into English as ". . . and all the Fulani he saw he [could not] <u>but kill them</u>, [sparing] <u>neither the learned nor the ignorant, neither men nor women.</u>" Yet, Wise and Hala AbuTaleb translate it as "He could not look at a Fulani <u>without killing him</u>, *even if he or she was under the protection of a family that was not Fulani*" [our italics]. And, again, they fail to alert the readers to the discrepancy between this and what was written by Houdas and Delafosse.

As far as one can see, Wise and Hala Abu Taleb's rendering of the end of the sentence has no support whatsoever in either the Arabic text or the French translation. However, if they believe they have made a legitimate breakthrough in the understanding of the Arabic original, they should not hide their success. They should instead let the rest of us know how they achieved it. Otherwise, confidence in the reliability of their entire translation of *TF* will remain seriously undermined, and one will sense in their work a lack of respect for its readers and, above all, for the Arabic text Wise's "Introduction" appears to treat with reverence (p. xxvii):

---

[7] In the phrase, the letter *qāf* at the beginning of the second word is written as ڧ instead of ق, following the Maghribian conventions adhered to in the Arabic text.

> The vision of history offered in the *Taʾrīkh al-fattāsh* is profoundly moral and even "contemporary," if read in comparison with the views of prominent philosophers, theorists, and theologians the world over.

Also, on p. 88 of their translation (corresponding to p. 44 of the Arabic text), which describes *Shī* Ali's assumption of political power, Wise and Hala Abu Taleb render the Arabic حصر بعضه ولي سلطنة سنغي as "He besieged the kingdom of the Songhay" (compare Houdas and Delafosse, p. 83: " Il fut investi de la royauté du Songaï"). Again there is a serious discrepancy between the French and English renderings of the Arabic phrase, but the readers are told nothing about it. Wise and Hala Abu Taleb's translation gives the false impression that *Sonyi* Ali was an outsider who came to power by means of a military conquest of Songhay. However, while حصر can indeed mean "to besiege," it is clear that it is used in this passage with another of its meanings, i.e., "to acquire," "to take for himself." In fact, just a few paragraphs before (p. 43 of the Arabic text, p. 81 of Houdas and Delafosse's translation, and p. 87 of Wise and Hala Abu Taleb's translation itself), *TF* states that *Shī* Ali "succeeded" (خلَف) *Shī* Silmān Dāmā, and makes clear that both belonged to the same series of rulers.

Had the present English translation of *TF* been based, as it claims to be, on a careful rereading of both the Arabic text and the French translation of the chronicle, Wise and Hala Abu Taleb would have spotted (and told the readers about) at least one mistake made by the French translators. On p. 152 of the Arabic text, at the beginning of line 10, Houdas and Delafosse misread العباد (*al-ʿibād*) as العبيد (*al-ʿabīd*).[8] Hence, on p. 272 of their French translation, at the end of line 11, they render the word as *esclaves* ("slaves"), instead of providing its correct translation ("servants of God," i.e., "the common run of Muslims and the people in general"). But on this point Wise and Hala Abu Taleb remain absolutely faithful to the French translation. They repeat the mistaken rendering "slaves" (p. 262, beginning of line 17), apparently without noticing that the Arabic text says something else. A misprint ("inequity" for "iniquity") compounds the mistranslation.

Elsewhere in the present English translation, a number of Houdas and Delafosse's footnotes to their French translation of *TF* have also been

---

[8] See P. F. de Moraes Farias, *Arabic Medieval Inscriptions from the Republic of Mali: Epigraphy, Chronicles, and Songhay-Tuāreg History* (Oxford: Oxford University Press for the British Academy, 2003), lxxv.

abandoned without informing the readers, while other footnotes remain but in a corrupt state. On p. 4, footnote 1 (compare Houdas and Delafosse, p. viii, footnote 1, of their original French "Introduction"), unacknowledged and misleading changes were inflicted on what the two French editors and translators wrote. The two final lines are dropped from the original footnote, and the French words *parti tiré* ("advantage taken") are mistranslated as "portion of the manuscript torn out." Hence, Wise and Hala Abu Taleb's footnote suggests that Seku Ahmadu suppressed part of a certain prophecy contained in *TF.* This is not at all what Houdas and Delafosse's original footnote says. It is also absurd, as it is known that the mentioned prophecy is a nineteenth-century forgery calculated to serve Seku Ahmadu's political interests. Of course he would not suppress any part of it. On the contrary, it was precisely under his auspices that the whole fake prophecy was added in the nineteenth century, together with other fabrications, to *TF*'s seventeenth-century text.[9] This glaring mistake confirms that Wise and Hala Abu Taleb are out of touch with the history of *TF*'s text, and that their readers will get no help from them on the subject. This is further confirmed by the fact that the readers are not alerted to Hunwick's deconstruction of an earlier, seventeenth-century forgery inserted in *TF.*[10] Wise and Hala Abu Taleb totally overlook Hunwick's paper, which is not even listed in their bibliography.

On page 170, footnote 15, line 1 (compare Houdas and Delafosse p. 174, footnote 1, line 1), Wise and Hala Abu Taleb again mistranslate French words. The expression *en effet* ("indeed") is rendered as "more or less," changing the meaning of what Houdas and Delafosse wrote.

Wise and Hala Abu Taleb's book does not disclose the transliteration rules it follows in the rendering of either Arabic or African-language words. In their own transliterations of Arabic and Arabicized personal names, Houdas and Delafosse carefully adhered to the Arabic rules concerning the use of the two different forms of the Arabic particle that means "son of" (*bin* or *ben,* often abbreviated in transliteration as "b.," and *ibn*). That careful stance is not replicated by Wise and Hala Abu Taleb, who indiscriminately use the form *ibn,* even where the Arabic text and the French

[9] On this see above all Levtzion ("Seventeenth-Century Chronicle," 573, 592), but also Houdas and Delafosse's French introduction to *TF* (xii), and its translation by Wise and Hala Abu Taleb itself (7–8). Levtzion clarifies the issue much further than Houdas and Delafosse's "Introduction" was able to do at the time it was written.

[10] Hunwick, "Studies in the *Taʾrīkh al-Fattāsh,*" part 2.

translation use *bin/ben* (see for instance pp. 170–71 of the present English translation, and compare pp. 92–93 of the Arabic text and pp. 174–75 of Houdas and Delafosse's original translation).

This vagueness about rules leaves one in doubt as to whether certain distortions of place names in Wise and Hala Abu Taleb are simply misprints or symptoms of a rather casual attitude toward transliteration. Thus, on p. 170, line 8, of the present English translation (compare p. 92, line 9, of the Arabic text), the middle و is ignored in the place name جَوْكَل (which may be rendered into English as "Jawkal"). The name is incorrectly rendered as "Diakal," not "Diaokal" (the somewhat better transliteration actually provided by Houdas and Delafosse in their original translation, p. 173, line 15). One of Houdas and Delafosse's footnotes (p. 173, footnote 8, of the original French translation) carefully gives the two alternative Arabic spellings of this place name in *TF*'s manuscripts. Unfortunately, like other Houdas and Delafosse footnotes that point to specific features of *TF*'s Arabic text, this particular footnote was regarded as redundant by Wise and Hala Abu Taleb, and they left it out. Had such footnotes been taken into account by the two writers, better transliterations might have been achieved by them for the benefit of their readers.

In the "Introduction" to his and Hala Abu Taleb's English translation (p. xi), Wise dismissively describes Dubois's book *Tombouctou la mystérieuse* as a "colonialist travelogue."[11] Yet much of his own "Introduction" reads as a wide-eyed travelogue along the Niger Valley between Timbuktu and Gao, and between lore about Qurʾānic prophets and legends about sorcerers and river spirits. It lavishes hyperbole on *TF* (pp. x, xxvii), but never engages with the necessary analysis of its rhetoric, nor with the way in which *TF,* like the *Taʾrīkh al-Sūdān,* contrasts with earlier Timbuktu scholarship. Hence it cannot really tell the readers about *TF*'s particular ideological slant on history, nor point out where the chronicle's literary originality lies. The "Introduction" is keen on the oral stories Wise heard in Timbuktu and Gao, but not at all keen on analytical approaches to such stories.[12]

[11] F. Dubois, *Tombouctou la Mystérieuse* (Paris: Flammarion, 1896), translated by Diana White as *Timbuctoo the Mysterious* (New York: Longmans, Green, 1896; reprinted New York: Negro Universities Press, 1969).

[12] Contrast Wise's stance toward these oral stories with the productive approach to oral evidence adopted by an author he cites (pp. xiii, xxi), Thomas A. Hale, *Scribe, Griot, & Novelist: Narrative Interpreters of the Songhay Empire* (Gainesville: University of Florida Press, 1990).

It contains a couple of howlers that do considerable disservice to its readers by feeding wrong information to them. On p. xi, it refers to "Fondo Kati, the present curator of the Kati family libraries in Timbuktu," as if "Fondo" were a personal name. Actually, *fondo* is a Spanish word that in this context means "library collection." "Fondo Kati" is the name of the Kaʿti family library in Timbuktu. It reflects the family's historical links with Spain.[13] The name of the library's curator is Ismaël Diadié Haïdara.

On p. xii, one is told that it was "the Pasha of Fez" who sent an army from Morocco to conquer Songhay.[14] In fact, the invading army was dispatched by Morocco's *Sulṭān* (who actually claimed the title of caliph) Aḥmad al-Manṣūr.[15] On p. xvii, Wise says that a story told him in Timbuktu about the staff of Prophet Mūsā (the biblical Moses) turning into a snake, which devoured the snakes into which the staffs of Pharaoh's sorcerers had metamorphosed, was "something I had never heard." But, in fact, this is far from being an unusual theme. Rather, it is widely known among West African and other Muslims, and among those who study either written texts or oral narratives generated by African Muslims. It is an elaboration of Qurʾan 20:69 and 26:44–45.

On p. xiii, Wise talks about "the Niger River, or the Djoliba ('River of Griots') as it is known in West Africa." In fact, the Niger River has different names in different languages of West Africa. Moreover, as noted long ago by Delafosse, its Manding name *Joli-ba* does not derive from *Jeli* ("griot"), but rather from *joli* ("blood").[16]

No map or alphabetical index is provided for the readers. It is difficult to overlook these, and other, fundamental flaws in Wise and Hala Abu Taleb's work so as to go along with Wise's statement (p. x) that

[13] See A. Hofheinz, "Goths in the Land of the Blacks: A Preliminary Survey of the Kaʿti Library in Timbuktu," in *The Transmission of Learning in Islamic Africa,* ed. Scott S. Reese (Leiden: Brill, 2004), 154–83. The library's present building in Timbuktu, inaugurated in September 2003, was erected with the help of Spanish financial support provided by the Andalusian regional government.

[14] The invasion happened in 1591, though Wise's "Introduction" fails to provide this chronological marker.

[15] See Dahiru Yahya, *Morocco in the Sixteenth Century: Problems and Patterns in African Foreign Policy* (Burnt Mill: Longman, 1981), 149; Zakari Dramani-Issifou, *L'Afrique Noire dans les relations internationales au XVIe siècle: analyse de la crise entre le Maroc et le Sonrhai* (Paris: Karthala, 1982), 116–23.

[16] M. Delafosse, *La langue mandingue et ses dialectes*, vol. 2 (Paris: Imprimerie Nationale and Librairie Orientaliste Paul Geuthner, 1955), 294.

> the modest goal of this book is to introduce an important but neglected document to the English-speaking world, in the belief that . . . the length of the present version will suffice for all but the specialist.

The English-speaking nonspecialist public expect, and deserve, better than they are getting with this publication.

P. F. de Moraes Farias, University of Birmingham

Georges Bohas, Abderrahim Saguer, and Bernard Salvaing, eds. *L'inspiration de l'éternel: Eloge de Shekou Amadou, fondateur de l'empire peul du Macina by Muḥammad b. ʿAlī Pereejo.* Brinon-sur-Sauldre: Éditions Grandvaux, 2011. 200 pp. €19.

As David Robinson observed in his study of ʿUmar Tall, "the historiography of the Central and Western Sudan has been dominated by the themes of long distance trade, state formation and islamization . . . It runs through the medieval states of Ghana, Mali, Gao-Songhay, Hausaland, and Kanem-Bornu, and then culminates in the *jihāds,* or holy wars, of the eighteenth and nineteenth centuries and the states which resulted from them."[1] Among the different postjihad states in West Africa the one that has attracted the least scholarly attention is by far the Fulani Empire of the Masina, also known as the Dina (from the Arabic word *dīn,* "religion"), or the Caliphate of Ḥamdallāhi (from the name of its capital)—from now on simply referred to as the "Caliphate."

The Caliphate, located in an area that belongs today to modern Mali, was founded in 1818 by Aḥmad b. Muḥammad Būbū al-Fulānī, better known as Aḥmad Lobbo (d. 1845).[2] The core of the state was the Masina region, situated in the inland Niger Delta, but at the peak of its power, the Caliphate claimed authority over an area spanning from the southern shores of the Sahara and town of Timbuktu to the latter's "twin city" Jenne, from northeastern Burkina Faso to the Malian city of Segu.

For a long time Hampaté Ba and Jacques Daget's classic *L'empire*

[1] David Robinson, *The Holy War of Umar Tal: The Western Sudan in the Mid-Nineteenth Century* (Oxford: Clarendon, 1985), 1.

[2] On Aḥmad Lobbo and his writings, see John O. Hunwick et al., *Arabic Literature of Africa IV: The Writings of Central Sudanic Africa* (Leiden: Brill, 2004), 208–13.

peul du Massina[3] and Bintou Sanankoua's monograph[4] were the only major contributions on the topic. These works are based on oral traditions. This represents a paradox, since both studies convey the notion that the spread of literacy in the Arabic language within the lands controlled by Ḥamdāllahi was one of the most relevant achievements of the Caliphate.

The recent *L'inspiration de l'éternel: Eloge de Shekou Amadou, fondateur de l'empire peul du Macina,* edited and translated by Georges Bohas, Bernard Salvaing, and Abderrahim Saguer, represents a first step toward a serious evaluation of the literary heritage of the Caliphate, a heritage that is still largely uncharted. *L'inspiration de l'éternel* is part of a larger project devoted to the study of the texts preserved in the Bibliothèques du Desert, the newly established VECMAS (*Valorisation et édition critique des manuscrits arabes sub-sahariens*).[5]

The VECMAS project, led by the well-known Arabist Georges Bohas, started in 2009 after an agreement between the École Normale Supérieure Lettres et Sciences Humaines of Lyon and the Mamma Haidara Memorial Library of Timbuktu. However, the team includes other scholars from different European and African institutions, such as Tal Tamari, Bernard Salvaing, and Seyni Moumouni. The aim of VECMAS is to produce critical editions of Arabic works from sub-Saharan Africa and the project has already published eight works—one in three volumes—some with both the Arabic text and the French translation and some with only the Arabic text. This is a most welcome addition to the African Islamic library.

Unfortunately, these publications neglect the material features of the manuscripts that contain the texts being edited and translated, confirming the argument that the bulk of the work done on West African manuscripts tends to satisfy the "thirst" of scholars for new sources that can cast light on the history and culture of Africa.[6] These studies are thus, in the words of Graziano Krätli, "conceived and implemented to serve literary interests and purposes. Therefore, they meet the expectations and the needs of literary scholars, but inevitably disappoint codicologists and other students of

[3] Amadou H. Ba and Jacques Daget, *L'empire peul du Macina, 1818–1853* (Paris: Mouton, 1962).

[4] Bintou Sanankoua, *Un empire peul au XIXe siècle: La Diina du Maasina* (Paris: Karthala, 1990).

[5] See the project website at http://vecmas-tombouctou.ens-lyon.fr/.

[6] Mauro Nobili, "Manuscript Culture of West Africa," forthcoming 2013.

the book as a material and technological object."[7] Indeed, a more holistic approach to the manuscripts, as both content and container, would further enrich the value of the VECMAS publications which represent nonetheless one of the major contributions to the study of the West African literary heritage in the last decade.

Among the first outputs of the VECMAS series, *L'inspiration de l'éternel* is a meticulous critical edition with the French translation of an elegy written to celebrate the founder of the Caliphate, Aḥmad Lobbo. The work is a hagiography in the *basīṭ* meter, titled in Arabic *Fatḥ al-ṣamad fī dhikr shayʾ min akhlāf shaykhinā Aḥmad* and written shortly after the death of Aḥmad Lobbo in 12 *Rabīʿ* I 1261/April 20, 1845. Its author is Muḥammad b. ʿAlī Pereejo, a son of a Muslim Kunari chief who pledged *bayʿa* (alliance) to Aḥmad Lobbo after the battle of Noukouma in 1818 which marks the beginning of the Caliphate.

The *Fatḥ al-ṣamad* consists of an introduction (*muqaddima*), seven chapters (*bābs*), and a conclusion (*khāṭima*). From the work emerges a hagiographic portrait of Aḥmad Lobbo which focuses on his virtues, asceticism, and knowledge, and the *baraka* he was bestowed with (*bābs* 1–6). It completely avoids all reference to Aḥmad Lobbo's important military and political efforts. The *Fatḥ al-ṣamad* is a work imbued with *Taṣawwuf* (Sufism) without any reference to *ṭarīqas* (brotherhoods), notwithstanding the general agreement of scholars that Aḥmad Lobbo was affiliated to the Qādiriyya. The Sufi background in which the work is framed in the introduction is that of the founders of *Taṣawwuf,* with explicit references to al-Ghazālī (d. 1111) and indirect allusions to Ibn ʿArabī (d. 1240). Furthermore, the work makes several references to later Andalusian and North African scholars, most of whom belong to the Shadhiliyya, confirming the intuition of Constant Hamès that the latter *ṭarīqa* might have influenced West African Islam well before the eighteenth and nineteenth centuries—the period usually associated with the initial spread of Sufi-oriented Islam in West Africa.[8] *Bāb* 7 and the *khātima* seal the work with a series of poems written during Aḥmad Lobbo's life or shortly after his death.

[7] Graziano Krätli, "Camel to Kilobytes: Preserving the Cultural Heritage of the Trans-Saharan Book Trade," in *The Trans-Saharan Book Trade: Manuscript Culture, Arabic Literacy and Intellectual History in Muslim Africa,* ed. Graziano Krätli and Ghislaine Lydon (Leiden: Brill, 2011), 329.

[8] On this topic, see Constant Hamès, "La Shâdhiliyya ou l'origine des confréries islamiques en Mauritanie," *Cahiers de recherche du Centre Jacques Berque* 3 (2005): 7–19.

Muḥammad b. ʿAlī Pereejo's work is preceded by an erudite *présentation* which represents a fundamental guide to reading the *Fatḥ al-ṣamad.* But the introductory essay goes beyond the text itself, locating the work in the intellectual milieu of West Africa and comparing it with other similar works, i.e., the biographical-hagiographical entry on al-Sanūsī (d. 1490) included in the *Nayl al-ibtihāj* by Aḥmad Bāba (d. 1627) and the *al-Ṭarāʾif wa-l-talāʾid* by Muḥammad b. al-Mukhtār al-Kuntī (d. 1825–1826).[9] Furthermore, the editors provide an accurate synthesis of the previous studies on the Caliphate which benefits substantially from two unpublished Ph.D. dissertations, by William A. Brown and by the Malian scholar Muḥammad Diagayété,[10] that are difficult to access, but crucial for any study on this topic.

In sum, *L'inspiration de l'éternel* is an important contribution to our still limited historical and literary knowledge of the Masina Caliphate, a state that has long been overshadowed by its more famous neighboring centers, Timbuktu, Sokoto, and the Tukuleur "empire" of ʿUmar Tall. The edition and translation of *L'inspiration de l'éternel,* as well the introductory essay, locates the work in the path of those great scholars who have disclosed to a wider public the first works of West African Arabic literature, such as Octave Houdas between the nineteenth and the twentieth centuries or John O. Hunwick later on.

Mauro Nobili, University of Cape Town

Cleo Cantone. *Making and Remaking Mosques in Senegal.* Leiden: Brill Academic Publishers, 2012. xliv, 436 pp.; 6 maps, 6 figures, 161 photographs. $182.00.

Making and Remaking Mosques in Senegal begins by presenting historical maps of the country of Senegal and Dakar city, its modern-day capital, along with figures of the mosques, women's spaces, and the different zawiyas (Sufi gathering places) of Dakar contributed by the distinguished

[9] On these works, see Hunwick et al., *Arabic Literature of Africa,* 27 and 113.

[10] William A. Brown, "The Caliphate of Hamdullahi (ca. 1818–1864): A Study in African History and Tradition" (Ph.D. diss., University of Wisconsin, 1969); and Muhammed Diagayété, *Al-Fulāniyyūn wa-ishāmuhum fī al-ḥaḍāra al-islāmiyya bi.Mālī* (Ph.D. diss., Zaytuna University, 2007).

geographer Eric Ross. These geographical mappings draw the reader's attention to the importance of Senegal's historically geostrategic location on the Sahelian and Saharan routes. Author Cleo Cantone is preoccupied with delineating the "links between architecture, gender, and identity, how they play one off against the other and how they transform areas of discourse through the medium of built form" (p. 15).

This book is an outstanding survey of the historical and social motifs that characterize Senegal's Islamic architecture. Cantone adopts an approach that is neither overly defensive nor Orientalist. She successfully synthesizes the constructions of Muslim identity in a diverse and multiethnic nation by exploring facets of Muslim Senegalese identity through the lens of mosque architecture. The varieties and intertextualities of contemporary mosque architecture arose from a history of amalgamating various styles. The author traces precolonial styles in Islamic architecture through colonial-era mosques, then details the modern and contemporary art of making mosques in Senegal. At the end, she highlights the versatility of the architecture and demonstrates women's agency in creating space within mosques.

Employing a chronological socio-architectural approach, Cantone traces Sudanese architectural styles and their counterparts in Futa Toro from the fifteenth to mid-nineteenth centuries in chapter 1. She discusses the precolonial trading ventures of Europeans in Senegal and highlights the architectural typology of the Umarian mosques, which date to the mid-nineteenth-century era of al-Hajj Umar. The stylistic construction of Umarian mosques relates to the broader family of Sudanese mosques, a building tradition going back several centuries. It is noteworthy that these mosques have a military demeanor that manifests a material expression of opposition to European intervention and domination. Due to scant references to this period, Cantone employs "European travelogue and an ethnolinguistic analysis to differentiate the various ethnic groups, their geographical setting and the distribution of local nomenclature to identify specific mosque types" (p. 21). This methodology draws more heavily from colonially generated descriptions than the indigenous historiography in which Muslims describe their mosques on their own terms.

The book's second chapter is a critique of the French colonial phase and its impact on the architecture of mosques in Senegal as well as on the formation of modern Senegalese identity. European intervention in Africa created several binaries: "inferior" African versus "superior" European, "Northern" versus "Sub-Saharan" African, and "white Islam" versus

"Islam Noir." Cantone demonstrates how these binaries manifested themselves in the French colonial approach to mosque construction in Senegal. For instance, the original mosque of Serigne Ndakarou was constructed with indigenous straw technique but was later substituted with a brick building, likely due to a French ban on perishable materials. Additionally, French authorities sought inspiration for the construction of Saint-Louis and Dakar mosques not in local prototypes but in a "hybrid style" that combined elements of Christian architecture with elements of North African and Arabian architectural traditions, considered more "civilized" than the indigenous "Islam Noir" building traditions. The church-like appearance of the two aforementioned mosques constitutes a concrete expression of French assimilationist ideology. Assimilation policy was based on a sense of colonial superiority, asserting that all people are hypothetically equal but that European and French civilizations are superior. Church-like traits such as the whitewashed exteriors and the clocks on the left-hand "minaret" towers of colonial mosques reflect this process by which the French aesthetic permeated African self-expression.

In the third chapter, Cantone continues to trace how shifting French colonial policies resulted in changing approaches to colonial mosque architecture. From the 1920s to the approach of independence in 1960, the colonial administrators in Senegal realized that it was in their best interest to collaborate with African chiefs to establish a sense of order and security between the locals and the colonialists. Hence, the objective of the French "mission civilisatrice" shifted in these years from cultural assimilation to cultural association. Corresponding to this move away from assimilation, French-sponsored mosques began to incorporate more neo-Moorish elements, in search of what the French considered an appropriate "African aesthetic."

Following the end of French colonialism, Senegal celebrated the ardor of independence in 1960. Cantone opens her fourth chapter by stating that these years witnessed the building of the Great Mosque of Dakar. This phase marks a conscious attempt at the Islamization of architecture in Senegal. The style, skills, and labor were all imported from Morocco. For this reason, the architectural style of mosques in the Tijani spiritual capital of Fez are reflected in the styles found at the local Tijani capital of Tivaouane in Senegal. The author also highlights the emergence of a new phenomenon: the Sunnification of mosques, a phenomenon transnationally imported to Africa by Wahhabi influence and locally known as producing "Ibadou" mosques. Thus, Cantone sheds light on another facet of

Islamic architecture and analyzes its repercussions in the construction of Senegalese Muslim identity. Cantone construes the mosque as a mirror of people's identity:

> Muslim communities of a given religious or ethnic affiliation express their identity through the construction of a mosque; in turn, the various elements of mosque construction, such as patronage, funding and social organization play a part in making the mosque a place of worship, in the sense of a place that embraces a confluence of different generations, their class, ethnic backgrounds and gender. (p. 238)

Hence, she correlates sources of funding with the diverse affiliations of the mosques. For example, the Ibadou mosques are influenced by Wahhabi Saudi style because this is their source of funding. Thus, the proliferation of mosque-building and the corresponding "international Islamic style" that has emerged in the last two decades is a phenomenon that goes hand in hand with the renewed wave of Islamization in Africa, also known in the Arab world as *islah* (reform).

The issue of allocating equal spaces to women and men in mosques is very often overlooked in gender studies and Islamic studies. The fifth chapter focuses explicitly on women in mosques, shedding light on a previously obscure topic. Cantone challenges stereotypes of Muslim women as mute, passive, and subordinate by showing how women wearing the hijab enthusiastically visit the mosque. Here Cantone demonstrates how women have appropriated and contested this space, particularly in the last two decades. She focuses on the reformist Ibadou women in an attempt to provide a counterbalance to the predominant focus on Sufi Islam—not only in the realm of Islamic architecture but also in the field of gender and Islam in West Africa.

This book discusses the relationship between gender and art, and their role in contributing toward a holistic African Muslim identity. As an art historian, Cantone adopts a unique approach toward investigating the architecture of mosques and how women negotiate their space in these mosques. She touches on numerous issues that influence the interplay of gender and Islam in a majority Muslim country like Senegal. She also converses with and sometimes refutes Paul Marty's Orientalist concepts of Islam in West Africa as emphasized in his book *Études sur l'Islam au Sénégal.* Cantone's book is a resourceful case study on Muslim women and their agency or lack thereof, and their negotiation of their own spaces in Senegal. The incidental personal anecdotes of Cantone's encounters with locals and her observations of Islamic practices from the perspective of a Muslim convert render the author's thesis graceful, genuine, and convincing.

The one identifiable weakness of the book is the writer's failure to document women's space in traditional Sudanese-style mosques as well as the "colonial mosques." The first four chapters incorporate little or no discussion of women's agency during those critical times in Senegal. The author does make a feeble effort to explore Muslim women's agency in the precolonial and colonial periods through mosque architecture, but only begins to discuss women's space specifically later in the book when she introduces the postindependence and contemporary mosques such as Markaz Bilal in the city of Thies. In this regard, women and gender issues that characterize a Muslim-majority country are not given sufficient attention, and Cantone might be accused of defaulting to an approach that she herself decries at the outset of the book. Although the final chapter is dedicated to women's spaces, the book would have preferably integrated the complexities of gender dynamics at every historical phase. While the writer proves to be critical of the Ibadou style of living in Senegal and their predominantly patriarchal exclusive architecture, she highlights the Ibadou female activism and participation in spreading Islamic teaching.

The architecture of Senegalese mosques proves an effective medium through which to communicate the different historical phases that fused to produce contemporary Muslim identity. In summary, *Making and Remaking Mosques in Senegal* places the art and architecture of Muslims within the sociopolitical context of the relationships between Muslim tariqas, numerous Islamic affiliations, and various ethnicities. The data presented and analyzed by Cantone serves as a thorough guide to the gender dynamics of Muslim worshippers in Senegal.

Naglaa F. Mahmoud Hussein, Howard University

Margot Badran, editor. *Gender and Islam in Africa: Rights, Sexuality, and Law.* Washington, D.C.: Woodrow Wilson Center Press and Stanford, Calif.: Stanford University Press, 2011. 336 pp. $60.00.

In most African countries, issues of religious pluralism and ethnic diversity pose persistent problems in the development of democratic and inclusive institutions in the postcolonial nation-state. One of the most contentious issues has been the assurance of equality of rights between men and women and the respect for religious diversity and their diverse views on issues regarding gender and the family. Similar debates have occurred in predominantly Muslim states as they attempt to determine the proper role of Islamic traditions about women and the family within the context of various types of nation-states. Regardless of whether Islam represents the majority of the population or a minority, Muslim organizations have sought to have their traditions regarding women, marriage, and the family recognized and respected within independent African states.

Given the salience of these issues from Morocco to South Africa, Margot Badran has served the academic community well by providing a rich collection of essays focused on the role of Islam in shaping women's rights, the institutions of marriage, and the role of family law. She has assembled important essays by both scholars of Islam in Africa and scholarly leaders in the campaign to assert gender equality within the context of Islamic traditions. The authors also reflect a variety of academic disciplines ranging from law to anthropology, religious studies, history, and literature. It is refreshing to see the discussion extended across the Sahara, demonstrating many similarities in issues relating to gender and Islam throughout the continent. Perhaps more importantly, it avoids the assumption that colors so much of the writing about Islam in Africa, that this is a frontier of the Islamic world dominated by syncretic forms of religious innovation. Many of the essays connect developments in countries like Gambia and South Africa with similar issues in South Asia or the United States. This anthology demonstrates that African Muslims are debating similar kinds of issues in regard to Islam, gender, and their newly independent states, that are being debated throughout the Muslim world. If there is an omission here, it would be the lack of coverage of the important East African states of Kenya, Tanzania, and Uganda which would have added to the anthology's breadth.

The anthology begins with a contribution from Beverly Mack, who has written extensively on the writings, teachings, and piety of Nana Asmaʾu dan Fodiyo of the Sokoto Caliphate in the nineteenth century. Although it treads familiar ground, it provides an important historical depth to other studies of Muslim women assuming educational leadership roles in the colonial and postcolonial eras. Continuing within a Hausa context, in Niger, Ousseina Alidou provides a fascinating account of Malama Aʾishatu Hamani Zarmakoy Dancandu, who became an important Islamic educator on Nigerian television and radio in the 1990s, based on her knowledge of Arabic and Hausa poetic texts, very much in the tradition of Nana Asmaʾu. Denied access to schools that combined French and Islamic learning, she emphasized the importance of women's education for the intellectual and spiritual growth of children and of the importance of both secular and religious studies.

Shifting to debates about the idea of an Islamic feminism, Raja Rhouni analyzes the works of Fatima Mernissi, in regard to her increasing engagement with Islamic perspectives on the equality of women. She traces Mernissi's shift from what Rhouni calls a secularist approach in which Islam is seen as essentially opposed to women's rights, which she would associate with Mernissi's early work, to an Islamic feminist position in her 1987 work, *Le harem politique: Le Prophète et les femmes.* In this work, she insists on expanding Qurʾanic exegesis to include an incorporation of the social context of seventh-century Arabia. Rhouni relates Mernissi's works to other Islamic scholars committed to the defense of gender equality on Islamic grounds, such as Amina Wadud and Asmas Burlas in the United States. Another case of an Islamic feminist perspective, by Rhouni's definition, is Saʾdiyya Shaikh's essay "Embodied *Tafsir,*" which discusses the issue of domestic violence in South Africa. She begins with a presentation of the Qurʾan's primary passages related to marriage. She focuses on the "Chapter on the Woman" (4:34), which raises a number of questions about the nature of the family and the relationship between husbands and wives. The assertion of the male as the senior partner and the problem of how to deal with unruly wives have been particularly troublesome for Muslim women committed to gender equality. She cites a number of scholars' treatment of the passage, Abu Jafar al-Tabari (839–922) and two scholars writing in the twelfth century. Although all three accept the idea of men as "protectors and maintainers of women," they disagree about what that means or the reasons for it. Only Abu Qasim al-Zamakshari accepts the idea that men may use physical violence against disobedient women. Al-Tabari and al-Razi insist that it should only be used as a last resort, never severely, and that the use of violence against women is not acceptable in the Islamic community. Having established a range of perspectives by classical jurists, Shaikh turns to what she calls embodied *tafsir,* Qurʾanic exegesis based on the life experiences of eight South African Muslim women who had experienced domestic abuse. Their experience of a God who opposed violence led them to reconstruct "their sense of self, of Islam and of Islamic ethics" (p. 112).

This theme of reconstructing ideas of gender and sexuality is emphasized in the second section of the anthology. Lidwien Kapteijns analyzes the debate about the role of women in the Somali nation-state as it is played out in Somali popular songs during the first four decades since independence. Marloes Janson provides a striking example of the way that Gambian Muslims, both men and women, adapted the missionizing work of the Tabligh Jamaʾat, which originated in South Asia, to a West African environment. They emphasized the role of married men and women, together going on missionizing tours in which they encouraged Muslims throughout the region to embrace a more "authentic" form of Islamic practice. The emphasis on women teaching women stood in sharp contrast to Jamaʾat practice in Pakistan and Bangladesh. Margot Badran's own contribution focuses on the Nigerian controversy over *hudud* punishments for extramarital relationships, in which two women were sentenced to death by stoning while their male partners were not even charged. Badran separates the largely ineffective outcry of the world community from the very skillful ways in which Nigerian women, both Muslim and Christian, worked within a shariʾa court system to overturn the initial verdict.

The last group of essays focuses on the complex issues involved in reforming the family law codes of predominantly Muslim states and the effort to obtain legal recognition of Muslim family law in a secular, egalitarian society of postapartheid South Africa, in which issues of religious freedom conflict with legal mandates for gender equality. Corinne Fortier examines Mauritanian marriage traditions in which monogamy was the accepted norm, but in which commercial traders, herders, and other migrant laborers often entered into secret marriages away from home. The essay concludes with the use of Islamic law by first wives, who had guarantees of monogamous marriages in their marriage contracts, to assert sole rights of inheritance and other forms of legitimacy by appealing to Malikite legal traditions. Julie E. Pruzan-Jorgensen describes the difficult process of family law reform in Morocco, in which royal power was invoked to make limited reforms, making it difficult for women's groups to press for full equality. Benjamin Soares examines a similar case in Mali, in which broad reforms of family law to ensure gender equality became politically unviable in the face of broad Muslim opposition, not because they opposed all reform, but because the reforms did not provide legal status for marriages contracted by religious authorities without formal registration of such marriages with the government. Finally, Rashida Manjoo examines the ongoing controversy that both the apartheid government and the independent South African governments refused to recognize Muslim marriages. Under apartheid, the government opposed Muslim marriages, because they made a space for polygynist marriages. Postapartheid South Africa continues to study the ways in which the religious freedom that Muslims should be able to enjoy in South African can be reconciled with constitutional mandates for gender equality.

This is an important collection of essays, which challenges the ideas of a homogenous African Islam, while also showing the ways in which Muslim women are challenging patriarchal concepts of society and the family within the context of various types of "embodied," historically contextualized interpretations of the Islamic tradition. It places African Muslim debates about gender and family firmly within the greater Islamic context while respecting the specific situations of various African countries.

Robert M. Baum, Dartmouth College